# BLACK COUCH CONVERSATIONS

## Let's Talk About Black Love

Catrice M. Jackson, MS, LMHP, LPC
(Nyalla Mkale Ukwazi)

Published by Catriceology® Enterprises, LLC
Omaha, NE | United States of America
Copyright © 2021 by Catrice M. Jackson (Nyalla Mkale Ukwazi)

The author has made every effort to ensure the accuracy of the information within this book was correct at the time of publication. The author does not assume and hereby disclaims any liability to any party for any loss, damage, or disruption caused by errors or omissions, whether such errors or omissions result from accident, negligence, or any other cause.

This publication contains the opinions and ideas of its author and other third parties. It is sold with the understanding that neither the author nor the publisher is engaged in rendering medical, health, psychological, or any other kind of personal professional services in the book. If the reader requires personal, medical, health, or other assistance or advice, a competent professional should be consulted. The author and publisher specifically disclaim all responsibility for any liability, loss, or risk, personal or otherwise, that is incurred as a consequence, directly or indirectly, of the use and application of the contents of this book.

This is a work of non-fiction. However, certain names and details have been omitted or changed, some characters are composites, and dialogue has been edited.

**FOR INFORMATION CONTACT**
Catrice M. Jackson (Nyalla Mkale Ukwazi), MS, LMHP, LPC, America's #1 Expert on White Woman Violence, Racial Justice Educator, Speaker, and International Best-Selling Author.

**ONLINE ORDERING IS AVAILABLE FOR ALL PRODUCTS**
www.amazon.com

**WEBSITES**
www.catriceology.com
www.shetalkswetalk.com
www.catriceologyenterprises.com
www.justiceislovecoalition.com

ISBN-13: 978-0-9838398-9-7 (Catriceology® Enterprises, LLC)

Book Cover Design: Kerri Liu
Interior Design: Kerri Liu
Editor: Marian Gallagher

Printed in the USA 10 9 8 7 6 5 4 3 2

# BLACK COUCH CONVERSATIONS

## Let's Talk About Black Love

Catrice M. Jackson, MS, LMHP, LPC
(Nyalla Mkale Ukwazi)

# Table of Contents

# Dedication

*This book is dedicated to my grandchildren,*
*Tyson, Tahlia, and Tytan*

May love be your constant fuel, fire, fortitude, and fortress in your quest for personal and communal justice, freedom, liberation, and Black joy! Let love be the torch you carry to illuminate the path of your love revolution. And above all else… love and be love despite your Beautiful Struggle. Never forget: Black love is beautiful!

I love you beyond eternity,
Nana (aka Nyalla MKale Ukwazi)

# Preface

This is not your ordinary book about love. This book was written for Black people, melanated people of the African diaspora. This book is about Black love, the beauty and the struggle of Black love. It is not a book about infatuation or romance; it is not a book about how to fall in love or land your dream relationship. Of course, those moments are part of love, but this book is about something deeper, more meaningful, and enduring. It's about Rafiki (Friendship) Love, Kinship (Community) Love, Romantic Love, and Soul Love. The kinds of love Black people need to survive and thrive. I'm talking about *revolutionary* Black love!

You won't get all hot and steamy reading this book, unless you are turned on by truth and power. You won't escape into a lustful wonderland, and you won't be overwhelmed by a fanciful fairytale about meeting your soulmate and living happily ever after—although I hope you are inspired to open your heart wider to fully and passionately give and receive Romantic Love. I am certainly no love expert. But everything I do is rooted in love, Black love, so I'm sharing my perspective on what love is and how to give and receive it. Most importantly, this book will take you on a deeper journey of *self-love*. A straightforward journey with raw truth, real talk, and practical solutions and strategies to move further away from fear and cynicism and closer to real and lasting love.

This book is an illustration and celebration of Black love and its Beautiful Struggle. Love is not perfect. It is not without pain, because it takes courage and vulnerability to love yourself and others. Love is a risky gamble. And when you say yes to love, you let down your guard and open yourself up to the possibility of both pain and pleasure. That is the risk you take for love.

This book was written for Black people. Black people who want to learn how to love and honor themselves more, and how to love on each other in deeper and more meaningful ways. This book is for Black people who want to use love as a tool for justice, freedom, and liberation. Who want to use love to help them return to themselves. Who want to embrace and embody love as the armor for a collective win against the forces trying to silence and strangle us! Against the forces of white terrorism that plot to suffocate Black love.

This book is for you, Black People. I hope it inspires you to use love as a healing balm. And I hope it empowers you to be not only radical about self-love but also revolutionary in your love for Black folks everywhere. It is true: We all we got! So, let's get to loving each other. Our revolution is love. Let us win together!

Asé!

# Introduction

Love. It is perhaps one of the most misunderstood, misused, and abused emotions known to humankind. Precious. Both delicate and mighty. Love. A mysterious phenomenon often eluding the very people who desperately seek its comfort and consumption. Love is ubiquitous and infinite. There is as much love available to you as there is air to breathe. Unfortunately, many people hold their breath as they wait for love to resuscitate them. They fail to realize all they have to do is inhale and let love rescue them from themselves. This truth sounds whimsical and ambiguous. It is not. Love is not avoiding us; we are avoiding it. Why? Because of fear.

Are you afraid of love? Perhaps you are and don't realize it. We either love or we don't. We're either in love or we're not. We're either loving or we're not loving. You may think this perspective is black and white, and it is. The truth is, we are acting either from love or fear, and any action in between lies in the gray area of inaction or indecisiveness. In the gray area between love and fear there are shades of gray that show up as doubt, cynicism, and grief, among other feelings and emotions. There is nothing wrong with these shades of gray. They are a natural part of our human expression. But they mean you are not choosing love. Emotions in gray are "pulling away" responses, rather than the "moving toward love" and/or "actively loving" emotions you probably yearn for. And when you avoid, refuse, and/or pull away from love, you are experiencing a fear response.

Love is a verb, which means it requires loving movement and loving action. Doubt, cynicism, and grief are feelings that take you further away from love. Trepidation is not love. Despair is not love. Dread is not love. Instead, these are other words for fear and the other shades of gray. Grief impedes love. Grief is the mask we wear to cover up pain, anguish, sorrow, and suffering. Grief has been described as love with nowhere to go. Love with no one to love. Grief is a filter for how we feel and engage with others; thus, it doesn't allow us to give and receive the full intensity and magnificence of love. Grief puts up a barrier and causes love to be stagnant. But love is not inert. It is not static, lifeless, or immobile. If you're experiencing these passive states… you're certainly not feeling love. You're probably feeling fear. When you peel back the layers of grief, doubt, trepidation, and cynicism about love… you will find fear. Fear that causes you to hold your breath… about love.

But there is excellent news! You can exhale and remove the filter of fear when you better understand what love is and is not. You can exhale and allow yourself to love when you decide what love looks like and feels like for you. I believe the media, fairytales, celebrities, and Hollywood often paint unrealistic and unattainable pictures of what love looks like, whether it be romantic or platonic love. And when we fail to create what is depicted and determined by others, we feel like we are failing at love. One reason I wrote this book is to empower you to take control of not only how you define love but also how you choose to give and receive it. I especially hope to empower you to take control of how you choose to love yourself and your fellow Black people.

Love is the breath in life's lungs. Take it in, and let love revitalize your cells. Every single magnificent molecule. You deserve it. In this book, I'll describe your *deserve level* and its use as a measure of what you believe you are or are not worthy of. I share strategies and action steps to help you determine and raise your deserve level. Doing so will allow you to experience love's full range of motion in romantic and platonic relationships, as well as with your fellow Black community members. I also focus quite a bit on self-love, because the inability to love yourself prevents you from giving and receiving the love you deserve. And because love is action, you'll learn how to create your definition of love, how to set expectations and boundaries for how you choose to be loved, and how to better express love toward intimate partners, friends, family, community members, and your Black siblings of the African diaspora.

This book is for Black people! Why? Because we are globally and collectively fighting the toxic forces of white terrorism and anti-blackness that want to silence, oppress, and kill not only our bodies but also our abilities and desires to love one another. Simply living in Black skin everywhere—but particularly in the United States—is stressful and often debilitating. This deadly force is known as white terrorism, aka toxic whiteness, and it seeks to destroy our joy, happiness, peace, passion, and yes, our love. It seeks to destroy our love of self, our love for others, and our love for the Black community. Toxic whiteness has been trying to suffocate Black love for centuries, using powerful weapons that kill Black bodies and wage spiritual warfare on Black minds and Black love. Our Kinship Love is under attack, and if we let whiteness

take or control our love, we won't win. Our love for one another is what has helped us survive. Love, Black love, is the revolution. It is and will be the love that arms us with the power to defeat the forces that want us subservient, oppressed, and dead. Love is our most potent weapon. Black love is the revolution that leads to our justice, freedom, and liberation. The revolution will be love. It's time to *amour up!*

So, come journey with me into an exploration of Black love. A journey that resists the urge to water down, glamorize, and mystify love. A journey where the concept of love is palatable and digestible. Let's talk about love in a way that allows you to metabolize it while gaining practical and tangible tips for taking off your filters. Without your filters of grief and fear, you can experience love in ways you never thought possible. Walk with me on a journey of self-love, and learn how to give and receive to *yourself* the love you deserve. And finally, journey with me into the Beautiful Struggle of Black love to embrace all its imperfections and glory.

I encourage you to not only read this book, but to also try the suggested activities. At the end of each chapter, I invite you to write a few Love Notes in response to the prompts I've provided. In addition, the Resources sections called "The Catriceology Way" and "Writing Prompts To Rise From the Ashes" include prompts. Use them to help you release and process your feelings around fighting both systemic racism and anti-blackness.

Love is rooted in action. Let's put your love in motion. Love is sacred. Love is redemption and restoration. Love is revitalizing and revolutionary. Exhale. Let love hold you and nurture you. Let love heal you and inspire you. Allow love to feed and nourish your mind, body, and spirit. Let it be your strength. Let love be the compass that returns you to yourself.

Above all else… love. Even when it is a Beautiful Struggle.

Inhale.

Exhale.

Let us begin this love journey together.

LOVE
BOMB

"A generous heart is always open, always ready to receive our going and coming. In the midst of such love we need never fear abandonment. This is the most precious gift true love offers — the experience of knowing we always belong."

bell hooks
*All About Love: New Visions*

# CHAPTER ONE

# Does Love Have a Brain?

*"To truly love we must learn to mix various ingredients —
care, affection, recognition, respect, commitment, and
trust, as well as honest and open communication."*

**bell hooks**

As I prepared to write this book, I asked myself: "*What if love has a brain? What would love think and feel, and why?*"

Let me note I am not a love expert. But because I am a licensed mental health professional, I know a lot about the psychology of human behavior. As an appreciator and practitioner of psychology, my brain is wired and trained to view the world and the way I move through it with a psychological lens. This skill is both intriguing and annoying. Intriguing, because I love examining the world through psychological eyes. Annoying, because I find it challenging to turn off my analytical brain. And when my analytical brain is *on*, I tend to psychoanalyze almost everything. It is bittersweet to have this gift and skill, because I long to "just be" when engaging with *certain* folks. However, I have a great ability to be present when I am intentional about it.

My perspectives on love stem from my professional training and knowledge, my personal experiences, and my curiosity. And when I declared LOVE would be my one word for 2021, I began thinking about love frequently. I also did some informal research (by reading articles, books, and scholarly papers) on the word "love," why people love, how

we love, and how love is embodied, avoided, and manifested. And hey, after being on this planet for half a century now, I believe I know a thing or two about what love is—and what it is not.

Humans have been trying to figure out love since forever. Although I will not go into great detail about this, I do want to mention a categorization of love first defined by the ancient Greeks and still popular today. They believed there were at least four kinds of love: Eros, Philia, Storge, and Agape:

- *Eros love* is passionate, sexual, and erotic love. It can be one-sided, as when one person feels Eros love for someone who does not reciprocate those feelings. Eros love is thrilling, exciting, and lustful. When two people feel Eros love for each other, it is dynamic and addictive, but it can also cause quite a bit of sorrow and grief.

- *Philia love* is essentially platonic love between two friends. When lovers have been together for a long time, they too may have Philia love for one another. This kind of love takes place between family members and is said to be good for your health, especially during hard times.

- *Storg love* is one of the most natural types of love. It is the love parents have for their children. Storge love is automatic, organic, and unconditional. Children do not have to earn this type of love; they are deemed automatically worthy of it.

- *Agape love* is selfless love and is given whether it is returned or not. Agape love is also called "the love of humankind," and is expected to be given unconditionally. Agape love does not judge and easily forgives.

So... what if love has a brain? Before we take a deep dive into the psychology of love, I will introduce the four kinds of love I will be highlighting in this book. These "love types" are ones I conjured up after synthesizing my research findings with my personal and professional experiences. My goals for this book are that it be digestible and intriguing. I don't want these love lessons to be overly philosophical or scientific. Often, we overcomplicate love, and although love *can* be complicated, it is also organic and simple.

But there are a few burning questions. Do we love with our brains or our hearts? Is it our hearts or our brains that fall in love? And which of those organs are doing the loving? Scientists are still debating the answers to these intriguing questions. I'll do my best to share what I discovered in my research on the topic. What is a heart, after all? Its primary purpose is to pump blood through our bodies to keep us alive. The heart has no memory—or maybe it does. It does not process thoughts or emotions—or maybe it does. At a fundamental level, the heart is an involuntary muscle that does the one thing it is designed to do: pump blood. But does it do more than that? I will continue to chip away at this debate of whether we love with our hearts or our brains. For now, let's explore the four general categories of love I've come with as a result of my informal research.

My four categories are *Rafiki Love, Kinship Love, Romantic Love,* and *Soul Love.* I will briefly describe these categories here, and then I will expand on Rafiki Love, Kinship Love, and Soul Love in upcoming chapters. You will see that I also emphasize self-love, because after all, this book is for you! I am not a Romantic Love expert, and the market is saturated with books about this most intimate type of love.

I want to travel a different path with this book: I want to take you on a journey through love. The topic of love is so overdone it has become bland. My hope is to add some psychological seasoning to spice up this conversation. While my names for the types of love may not be new or unique, I hope the way you digest my psychological flavor and perspective is both delectable and transformational.

In his song "Love," R&B singer and songwriter Musiq Soulchild alludes to the word and concept of love being used in vain. The song includes the line, *"Those who have faith in you (love) sometimes go astray."* My interpretation of these lyrics is that our issues with love are threefold: we frequently throw around the word "love"; we don't understand what the word really means; and we say it, but don't live it. Thus, love becomes hollow and futile. By the time you finish reading this book, I hope you'll learn how to make love more meaningful and authentic in your life, and I hope you will no longer use the word "love" in vain.

## Rafiki (Friendship) Love

Let's start with Rafiki Love. *Rafiki* means "friend" in Swahili. When I think about the friends I've loved most in my life, it is easy for me to see the special qualities of Rafiki Love. And while we all have differing opinions about the preferred qualities in friendships, the ones I will share are paramount to what it means to genuinely love platonic friends.

Here are seven critical elements of Rafiki Love and how I define them:

- *Mutual Respect:* To value each other's existence and presence through honoring and treating each other with dignity and care.

- *Admiration:* To approve, appreciate, adore, and be in awe of someone.

- *Authenticity:* To be genuine, transparent, and unrehearsed.

- *Integrity:* To be sincere and honest. To be who you say you are and do what you say you will do.

- *Trust:* To be trustworthy enough to be confided in. To be emotionally safe and to honor confidentiality.

- *Emotional Intimacy:* To allow others to be seen, heard, and emotionally validated and supported.

- *Honesty:* To tell the truth, be open, and speak with candor and compassion.

Other qualities may be more important to you, and that is perfectly fine. You may also have different definitions for the seven qualities I outlined, and that is okay too. There are no perfect prescriptions or definitions of friendship. I share my thoughts here as a basic template for the minimum you deserve in your friendships. In fact, there are more qualities I expect and require in my friendships, but these seven *must* be present as the foundation of my Rafiki (Friendship) Love. When these qualities and characteristics are consistently embodied and expressed by someone I call "friend," it allows for our relationship to solidify, expand, and flourish. When a person who considers themself my friend does not display these qualities in our engagements, it indicates they are not willing or able to love me the way I need them to.

## Kinship (Community) Love

When I think about the word "kinship," other words like "connectedness," "culture," "roots," "heritage," and "family" come to mind. Kin often refers to a familial bond or relationship. However, in a larger context, I believe kin expands beyond our biological and genetic ties. I have had many friends in my lifetime who felt more like family than some of my family members did. So, what causes non-family members to feel like family? If you have ever said, *"That person is the sister or brother I never had,"* then you know what Kinship Love feels like.

Kinship is also about affinity and being related through common ancestry. The love many Black activists (people) have for the collective Black community is Kinship Love. The love you and I feel for other Black folks in the struggle is Kinship Love. The way we Black people mourn the loss of stolen (murdered) Black lives—no matter where in the world those lives are lost—is Kinship Love. And because we share Kinship Love, we can love other Black folks in our collective community, but we may not like them or be in relationship with them.

So, where does this love come from, and what are its foundations? Here are seven critical elements of Kinship Love and how I define them:

- *Compassion:* To have deep feelings of tenderness, sympathy, and understanding of someone else's struggle or pain with a desire to alleviate their pain.

- *Affinity:* To have an organic liking for someone who shares your interests and/or desires.

- *Connectedness:* To be linked with another person on a soul level, anchored in shared ancestry.

- *Solidarity:* To be in alliance with someone who shares a common struggle or goal.

- *Acceptance:* To receive and honor others as they are.

- *Empathy:* To sense, understand, and share the feelings of others.

- *Altruism:* To be genuinely concerned for other people's welfare without ulterior motives, often at the risk of self.

Kinship Love can surpass differences, challenges, and disagreements. When you have Kinship Love for other Black people, you may not like or agree with them, but you share an ancestral affinity allowing you to feel empathy for their plight and/or be in solidarity with their difficulties and pain. I certainly do not like or agree with every Black person I know, yet there is one communal fiber fostering my love for them, because I empathize with their struggles. My story may be different from other Black folks' stories, but what we have in common is our need for—and our fight for—justice, freedom, and liberation. I believe we Black people can dislike each other, but still be in community and stand in solidarity with each other.

When I think about the Movement for Black Lives and Black Lives Matter, there is an innate kinship and affinity I feel for Black folks and those of the African diaspora. We Black people may reside in different chapters, yet our experiences are in the same book. I have encountered thousands of Black folks in my lifetime. I have met a variety of Black folks in the different cities I have traveled to. And no matter where I

go, when I engage with Black folks, there is some element of kinship or likeness. Their struggles may not be mine, but I have organic empathy and compassion for them. Over the years, I have ended friendships with Black people and/or distanced myself from them. But I hold no grudges against them. I do not wish them any harm. I do not plot their demise. I have simply released them with love, and I genuinely wish them well. And although we may not agree with or like each other for whatever reason, I can still be in community with them. I can love them from a distance, because I have an affinity for Black folks.

## Romantic Love

Romantic Love often oozes with deep passion, intense attraction, insatiable desire, and infatuation. It is exciting and exhilarating. It is hot and steamy. It can be lustful and endearing, especially in the beginning of a relationship. And sometimes Romantic Love can be addictive and heartbreaking. There are also moments of devotion, affection, and intimacy. Romantic Love has various shades and levels. It can be one-sided, and it does not always involve physical touch or sex.

I remember a time in the eighth grade when I was completely infatuated with a boy I'll call "Shawn." He was humble and quiet. He was fine! So fine that he was beautiful. I had the biggest crush on him, and he knew it. He appreciated the notes I would pass to him between classes. He was friendly and would talk on the phone with me for short periods. We never officially dated. I never touched him. But I felt a deep sense of connection with Shawn and an intense attraction for him. To be honest, I loved him. The love I had for him was appreciated, but it was not reciprocated. And that was heartbreaking. My crush on him

lasted well into the tenth grade or so, but eventually it went dormant on its own. If Shawn were still alive today and I were to bump into him, I'm sure my heart would still flutter a bit.

Romantic Love is intricate and textured. It can include robust emotional and physical connections. Romantic Love is tender, affectionate, and pleasurable. And because Romantic Love is one of the deepest and most profound types of love, we tend to throw our whole selves into it, which also puts us at risk for heartbreak, sadness, and sometimes anger and grief. I believe love is blind. And I believe this blindness can lead to intense and passionate everlasting love, or it can suck you into a place of great sorrow and despair when someone refuses or abuses your love. Romantic Love can be both exhilarating and hurtful.

Being romantically in love with someone is a risky gamble. You have no idea how that love thang is going to play out until you jump in with both feet and experience it for yourself. Nevertheless, I believe in love, and I believe in taking the risk to discover what love looks and feels like on all levels. And yes, I have felt pure exhilaration and infatuation in my romantic love relationships. Unfortunately, I have also experienced rejection, one-sided love, betrayal, and deep emotional pain in some of those relationships. At the end of the day, however, I will continue to choose love, because it is worth the risk. With more caution and discernment, of course.

You may have your own definition of Romantic Love, as we all should, but here are seven critical elements of Romantic Love and how I define them:

- *Attraction:* To have a strong interest, liking, or desire for someone that can be sexual, emotional, and/or physical.

- *Passion:* To have a powerful and compelling feeling for someone.

- *Devotion:* To be loyal and steadfast in your allegiance with someone.

- *Intimacy:* To sense or feel physical, emotional, and/or spiritual closeness.

- *Affection:* To have a tender and fond attachment to someone you like.

- *Desire:* To strongly want or crave to be with someone.

- *Vulnerability:* To be selfless. In other words, to intimately share your heart while knowing you risk having your feelings hurt.

**Soul Love**

Soul Love is unconditional, involuntary, and unmatched. The love that parents have for their children and vice versa are examples of Soul Love. Most times, a recipient of Soul Love does not have to earn it or prove their worthiness. It is automatic and natural. Soul Love is rich and rare. It's one of the most potent and pure kinds of love, and it is one of my favorites to give and receive.

I know this type of love well. Beyond the love I have for my mother, my first experience with Soul Love was love at first sight when my son was born. When I held him in my arms for the first time, that was my first experience of feeling unconditional, involuntary, and unmatched love. There was no other person in the world I loved like I

loved my son. And it was the first time in my life I knew there would be at least one person in the world who would love me unconditionally. I still believe that today.

Before I became a mother, I didn't have a deep understanding of my mother's love for me. After I gave birth, I realized the way my mother loves me is the way I love my son. Now I have the same kind of love for my grandchildren. Being a Nana is wonderful, because not only do I get to love my grandbabies, but I also get to love my son even more through loving them. And as much as I love my husband, the love I have for my seeds (my son and grandchildren) is a whole other intensity of Soul Love. It's perfect joy! It is infinite and abiding.

Soul Love can be indescribable, and it is not exclusive to family members. When you first meet certain people, your kindred spirits communicate on a soul level, and a familiar and cellular connection is ignited. I believe our souls know who our people are. The soul knows a kindred spirit when it encounters one. The soul knows who our spiritual kin is. You often hear folks talk about how you should find your tribe, aka the people who are meant to be in your life. You know those people who you just vibe and rock with, but you can't necessarily put your finger on why they are important? Those folks belong to your soul tribe. And when you have a lot in common with them, it is easy and organic to build relationships with them. Such people are rare and priceless, and if you encounter only one in your lifetime, it is a special gift. It is a blessing. When these kindred spirits show up in our lives, we need to know how to love them on a soul level, because a second chance may not be granted.

Here are seven critical elements of Soul Love and how I define them. I hope these definitions help you to *not* mess up the rare opportunity to love someone on a soul level:

- *Loyalty:* To be faithfully in allegiance with someone.

- *Reciprocity:* To engage in a mutual exchange of time, resources, feelings, and energy.

- *Gratitude:* To be thankful, and to consistently reciprocate acts of kindness.

- *Reverence:* To have deep devotion and respect for someone.

- *Affection:* To have a tender and fond attachment to someone you like.

- *Empathy:* To sense, understand, and share someone else's feelings.

- *Mutual Respect:* To value each other's existence and presence by honoring and treating each other with dignity and care.

Soul Love has a delightful characteristic called "chemistry." You meet someone, and there is an instant bond of comfort and familiarity. Your connection clicks and sparks, and you feel like you have known this person your entire life—or perhaps in a past life, if you believe in those. It's often difficult to explain this automatic connection, but you know it is real. You feel the affinity deep down in your bones. Your heart recognizes their heart, and sometimes you experience a literal or metaphorical exhale when your soul encounters their soul for the first time.

Soul Love is glorious! The people who I love on a soul level are some of my favorite people. They are my muses, my mirrors, my

confidants, and often my teachers, whether they know it or not. They challenge me to be a better person. They know my hopes, dreams, struggles, and desires, and sometimes without me even telling them. They know my heart. They can see past my facades into the deep hidden places inside. They love me beyond my titles, degrees, personality flaws, and possessions. Their soul loves my soul, and we have a significant amount of reverence, gratitude, respect, and affection for one another. And what's most important to me is they are more likely to consistently demonstrate loyalty and reciprocity.

Soul Love is not all unicorns and rainbows, though. Soul Love has its share of ups and downs, struggles, and challenges, just like any other kind of love. Soul lovers, soulmates, and soul friends are human. They are flawed and they make mistakes. Just because you have soul ties with someone does not mean they will not hurt you, let you down, or disappoint you. But in my experience, Soul Love relationships have greater empathy, compassion, and forgiveness. And I believe these relationship qualities come from the deep affection and reverence you have for one another. I also believe there is less ego and more unconditional regard involved in Soul Love. You consciously and subconsciously know how rare and priceless these types of people are, and so you are more deliberate with your actions and care.

Soul Love can be endless, but sometimes your soul people don't stick around for the long haul. Their departure does not diminish the legitimacy of the Soul Love; it just means their season is over in your life. Perhaps their season was to be your muse, guide, teacher, or healer for only a short time. Nevertheless, Soul Love is a beautiful blessing no matter its duration.

So, what if love has a brain? What would love think and feel, and why? I have had my heart broken many times in my life, and without a doubt, it is painful and paralyzing. I have even felt my heart hurting or throbbing with pain during those times. The anguish was unbearable. I didn't think I would emotionally survive some of those heartbreaks. Sometimes I could not sleep because I was so riddled with anxiety, and other times all I wanted to do was sleep away the despair. Other than sometimes having racing or grief-stricken thoughts, most of the pain I felt from those heartbreaks felt physically real—and it was. Aches and pains. Headaches and upset stomach. Loss of appetite or insatiable eating. These are all real manifestations of a broken heart. Many times I thought my heart was going to explode or stop beating. And while everything I just said is true, I wonder if it truly was my *heart* feeling, thinking, and hurting, or was it my *brain* feeling, thinking, and hurting, and it sent pain signals to my heart?

Some scientists say love comes from and feels like it originates in our hearts. Others believe love originates in our brains first and then our heart and mind become consumed with feelings of love. Here is a perspective to consider. In his 2019 article "Pain: Is It All in the Brain or the Heart?," Ali M. Alshami referred to the 1991 findings of Dr. J. Andrew Armour (a pioneer in the field of neurocardiology) about the heart's "little brain" as follows:

> *"Dr. Armour, in 1991, discovered that the heart has its 'little brain' or 'intrinsic cardiac nervous system.' This 'heart brain' is composed of approximately 40,000 neurons that are alike [sic] neurons in the brain, meaning that the heart has its own nervous system. In addition, the heart communicates with the brain in [sic] many methods: neurologically, biochemically, biophysically, and energetically. The vagus nerve, which is 80% afferent, carries information from the heart and other internal organs to the brain. Signals from the 'heart brain' redirect to the medulla, hypothalamus, thalamus, and amygdala and the cerebral cortex. Thus, the heart sends more signals to the brain than vice versa."*
>
> — Alshami, A.M. "Pain: Is It All in the Brain or the Heart?," *Current Pain and Headache Reports.* 23, 88 (2019).

This is interesting, and it is new information for me. Have you heard about this before? Let's keep peeling back the layers on the question of whether it is our brains or our hearts that feel love.

One definition of love is that it is an emotion comprising your attitudes, thoughts, feelings, and behaviors. And according to a 2012 article on the HeartMath Institute website, there is such a thing as "heart intelligence," which they define as *"... the flow of awareness, understanding and intuition we experience when the mind and emotions are brought into coherent alignment with the heart."* Our intellectual intelligence is often highly correlated with thoughts, reasoning, cognitive processing, and the ability to comprehend information.

Dr. Armour believes our heart sends cognitive and emotional signals to our brain to help us better govern our lives, it is in constant communication with the brain, and it makes many of its own decisions. One fact I found fascinating in Dr. Amour's research is that a fetus' heart starts beating before its brain is fully developed.

So, does love have a brain? Or perhaps it's better to ask whether love begins in our brains or in our hearts, and whether love resides only in our hearts without the functions of our brains. While the brain may have neurons and a nervous system, that doesn't necessarily mean the heart has a brain. As you can see, there are several perspectives and theories about whether the heart has a brain. I don't have a definitive answer, either. What I can say, however, is that love is anchored in the heart, often ruled by the heart, and definitely lives, manifests, flourishes, and can die in the heart. In my humble opinion, love does have a brain and it lives in the heart. And I believe love starts in our brains most of the time. I believe this to be true especially in Romantic Love. In Soul Love there is an immediate, effortless connection, but in Romantic Love, the process of "falling in love" is not always as automatic. In other words, in Romantic Love, sometimes the thoughts in our brain coerce us into loving with our hearts.

Love is wondrous and splendid! Love is attraction and fondness. Love is exhilarating and consuming. Love is respect, affinity, and passion. Love is patience and tenderness. Love is compassion, understanding, and kindness. Love is erotic, sensual, and sexual. Love is empathy, trust, and honesty. Love is complicated and intricate. Love is simple and pure. Love can be rare, priceless, and altruistic.

There are not enough words to adequately describe love, and the great news is we get to define it as we choose. We get to give it and receive it as we choose. Here are some things I know for sure:

- Love governs the way we think and feel about ourselves and others.

- Love determines how we perceive, engage with, and treat ourselves and others.

- Love allows us to be seen and heard.

- Love allows us to be held, understood, and cared for.

- Love is healing.

- Love is nourishment.

- Love is food for the soul.

Love is all this and more. Will you choose it every day? I hope you choose to give love and receive love. I hope you feed those you love with it. I hope you shower yourself with it and indulge in love daily. I hope you choose it first for yourself and then for others. It does not matter where love comes from. It does not need a fancy name. All that matters is you give it, and you allow yourself to receive it frequently, consistently, and abundantly!

## LOVE JUICE

*Love is... knowing your preferred Love Languages and asking those you love to love you the way you prefer to be loved, and to do the same for them.*

—*Catriceology*

## LOVE NOTES

How do you define love?

_____

_____

_____

_____

_____

Which type of love do you struggle giving and receiving the most
(*Rafiki Love, Romantic Love, Kinship Love,* or *Soul Love*)?

_____

_____

_____

_____

_____

What is your "heart brain" saying about love at this time in your life?

_____

_____

_____

_____

_____

LOVE
BOMB

"Kindness eases change.
Love quiets fear."

Octavia E. Butler
*Parable of the Talents*

# CHAPTER TWO

# Black Love: A Beautiful Struggle

*"I am grateful to have been loved and to be loved now and to be able to love. Because that liberates. Love liberates."*

**Maya Angelou**

**I Love Black People**

*I love Black people!*

> *Cornrows, twists, locs, and taper fades.*
>
> *Afro puffs and coils.*
>
> *Doo rags, Black Power fist picks, and hood swag.*

*I love Black people!*

> *Gospel music on Sunday mornings.*
>
> *Grits, collard greens, and sweet potato pie.*
>
> *Hip hop.*
>
> *The Harlem Renaissance.*
>
> *Rock and roll, doo-wop, R&B, and soul.*

*I love Black people!*

> *Snapbacks, dashikis, and bean pies.*
>
> *Lady Sings the Blues, the electric slide, and Langston Hughes.*
>
> *By any means necessary, Do the Right Thing, melanin poppin' Black Girl Magic, and that new jack swing!*
>
> *"Back That Thang Up," "Knuck If You Buck," black-eyed peas, and rolling trees.*

> Jumping the broom, Big Mama and nem, Cousin Ray Ray, and
> Training Day.

I love Black people!

> Multifaceted and multitalented innovative geniuses.
>
> Bringing flavor to everything.
>
> Kings and queens.
>
> Birthed from the cradle of humanity, rooted in the motherland,
> and first on all lands.
>
> No one does it like we do it, and it don't matter what "it" is.
>
> We salt of the earth.
>
> Fragments of the universe.
>
> Cosmic.
>
> Creative.
>
> Glorious.
>
> Naturally dope!

Black love, that's who we be.

> —Catrice M. Jackson

Yeah, it's safe to say I have Kinship Love for all Black people, everywhere! The ones I know and the ones I don't. The ones I am connected to and the ones I am not in community with. The ones I don't like, the ones who don't like me, and the ones who love me. I love all of them!

And yet, the world wants us to believe we are not worthy of love in all its fabulous forms and flavors. Not only does a global, anti-black agenda exist to make us believe we are not worthy, there is also a bounty out on Black love. To oppress and stop Black love by killing our bodies and silencing our spirits. Global anti-blackness is a vigorous

and treacherous pandemic, and it has been destroying Black people for centuries in every way possible. Anti-blackness is rooted in hatred and disdain, and it implies that Black people are inferior, unworthy, unlovable, and unimportant. Bullshit! I refuse to drink that poison.

This alleged, so-called "inherent Black inferiority" is a deliberate lie and dangerous myth baked into every global structure and system. Anti-blackness results in structural violence, social and racial injustice, discrimination, marginalization, global oppression, and exclusion. There is not a safe space or place for Black people in the United States. We can't shop, drive, vacation, dine, exercise, travel, learn, play, rest, gather, or sleep in our own beds without anti-black violence hunting us down to silence, oppress, and/or kill us. And it does. The bounties on our bodies are our struggle. One we must fight against every day. A struggle causing us to endure unnecessary spiritual and physical weathering. One that not only contaminates Black love but also stifles it.

There is a global, colonial force and spirit of toxic whiteness (aka white terrorism) lurking in every city, state, and country. This ferocious force and sinister spirit believes we Black people are not human, we are genetically inferior, and we are unworthy of sovereignty, justice, compassion, freedom, and love. This sick and twisted plot serves as the underbelly of a sociopathic plan to steal, maim, oppress, and kill Black bodies and spirits. Black people are under attack everywhere, and unfortunately, Non-Black People of Color (NBPOC) and some Black folks themselves are also contributors to this violence, whether they know it or not. Yes, this is true. I will expand on this truth in upcoming chapters, but if you want to better understand my perspective on this issue, get a copy of my book *Weapons of Whiteness™: Exposing the Master's Tools Behind the Mask of Anti-Blackness.*

With an insurmountable amount of anti-black violence attacking us daily, do we know what love is and how to create space for it? How do we expand our capacity for love? How do we give and receive love—not just mediocre love, but extraordinary and everlasting love? This is our Beautiful Struggle. And even when we know what love is, create space and capacity for it, and give and receive it, we still experience a Beautiful Struggle. Why? Because even our love is dehumanized and distorted. Historically, our bodies have been treated as property, cargo, and objects to experiment on. White people have regarded us as being more primitive than animals. Our bodies have been used, abused, and commodified for everyone's sadistic pleasure and economic profit. White folks have used Black women as breeding grounds and Black men as disposable sperm donors. We have had our joy beaten out of us, and we have been denied our human rights to pleasure and happiness. We have been conditioned not only to hate our own blackness but also to despise it in other Black people. Although Black love is resilient, it has been denied and contested by persecution, suppression, and aggression by everyone, including us. Loving in a Black body is a Beautiful Struggle.

The audacity of us to love is revolutionary! Despite the attacks against us, our choice and willingness to love are acts of resistance and persistence against the forces that want Black love to die. Black love is a Beautiful Struggle, because the magnificent intertwining of Black bodies is a majestic universe in motion. It's royalty mingled with royalty. It's regal. When kings and queens unite to form relationships

and unions, it is galactic. The universe beams with delight, because we are cosmic. Black love is celestial. When we show up in solidarity with one another and lock arms to defeat our giants, we are a powerful force to be reckoned with. The ground shakes because we are warriors. When we share intimate, vulnerable, and tender moments, the stars sparkle brighter, and our ancestors are overjoyed.

The audacity of us to love is life-giving and liberating. When we lay down the master's tools (aka anti-blackness) and build each other up instead of tearing each other down, we are unstoppable. When we can see past each other's pain and suffering and provide a safe place to release, there is peace. We are restored and rejuvenated. There is deep healing. It is love. A kaleidoscope of glorious Black love in motion. It is splendid! When we love, it is a spectacular work of beautiful art! We are love's sweet jewel.

I don't know about you, but when I see Black people loving on each other, my soul is ecstatic! And it does not matter what kind of love we are expressing; it is always revolutionary. It is a miracle we are even able to love after what our ancestors and the African diaspora went through and what we are currently enduring today. Not a day goes by in America when we are not reminded of the diabolical disdain whiteness has for us. Turn on the television and you will see it. Drive down the street and you will see it. Be in the wrong place and you will quickly sense it. Listen to the radio and you will hear it. Look into the eyes of whiteness, and you will feel it in their White Gaze (a Weapon of Whiteness™). You might be thinking, *"Catrice, I really don't care what white folks think."* Just know I don't care either. But in reality, their twisted perceptions of blackness fuel, govern, and execute the violent

systems and structures in which we live. Every single one. And that is our struggle. It is part of the struggle in our Beautiful Struggle.

Tamir Rice loved playing with his toy gun, and the wicked White Gaze took that love from him. Jordan Davis loved bumping the bass in his car, and the wicked White Gaze took that from him. Breonna Taylor slept in her own bed, in her own house with the man she loved, and the wicked White Gaze took that from her. White peoples' twisted perceptions and wicked White Gaze are threats to Black love. That is our struggle.

We cannot easily escape the gaze, because it is as natural and bountiful as the air we breathe. My definition of the White Gaze is *"[w]hen white folks stare at Black folks with violent curiosity, lust, and/ or disgust."* And this *looking* leads to white people experiencing false feelings of being threatened by our words and presence. Those feelings lead to them asking to speak to the manager, requesting security, and/ or calling the police. Some people may call this "white fragility," but to be honest, white folks' so-called fragility is not fragile… it's violent. It's manipulative and lethal violence. This gaze leads to traffic stops that lead to violence, incarceration, and murder. We have seen this relentlessly and repeatedly decade after decade.

We cannot escape the violent White Gaze, not even in our own homes. Korryn Gaines, Botham Jean, and Atatiana Jefferson were in their homes, and still the violent gaze penetrated their sacred and so-called safe spaces. The gaze does not allow Black people to do ordinary things. Amadou Diallo was standing outside his apartment building. Eric Garner was standing outside a store. John Crawford III was holding a BB gun in a Walmart. Philando Castile was a passenger in his

girlfriend's car during a traffic stop. Stephon Clark was holding a cell phone in his grandmother's backyard. When you have Black skin, it is a struggle to do normal, everyday things without the threat of violence.

Our struggle is multidimensional and unrelenting. Even for those of us who have "come up" or "made it," the struggle is real. Economic status, class, and/or financial success may ease some of the struggle, but it does not make Black people immune to racism, discrimination, or the manipulative violence of the White Gaze. Serena Williams could have died during childbirth due to systemic racism and medical anti-blackness. Because she has a history of blood clots, Serena told the (white) nurse that she might need a CT scan and blood thinner while in hospital. But the nurse did not take Serena's concerns seriously, chalking them up to Serena being "confused" by the pain medication. Despite Serena insisting on a CT scan with contrast, they performed an ultrasound of her legs. When the medical personnel finally performed the CT scan, they discovered several small blood clots in Serena's lungs. She was eventually put on blood thinners, but not until she insisted. Serena knew her body and her medical history, but it didn't matter. She still experienced medical gaslighting and could have died, lost her baby, or both. She ended up having an emergency C-section (more money for doctors), and her postpartum recovery was longer than normal.

I believe many non-Black doctors use our bodies to experiment on so they can increase their profits; thus, many unnecessary C-sections are prescribed for Black women. Regardless of their celebrity status, Black mothers are 243% (not a typo) more likely than white women to die of pregnancy- or childbirth-related causes. 243% more like *to die!* There is no safe place for Black people. Not even in the spaces that declare they are there to serve and care for all people. And especially not by those who claim their oath and duty is to protect and serve.

For the past five or six years, I have been accompanying my seventy-three-year-old mother to all her doctors' appointments because of medical racism. And this racism and anti-blackness are so innate and ingrained in the medical system that they (the white and NBPOC medical personnel) can't help but inflict it on her even when I am in the room. She has been accused of being addicted to pain medication when she requests it in the hospital. She has been denied pain medication until I called the medical personnel on their shit. Doctors have tried to push unneeded procedures and medications on her. The worst medical racism my mother faced was when her doctor ignored her complaints of numbness and toes that had turned black, even though she had a fifty-year history of blood clots and was on a prescribed blood thinner. Thus, all the toes on her right foot had to be amputated. I am one hundred percent convinced she experienced this because she is an elderly Black woman. This is our struggle.

The struggle does not stop there. The mass incarceration of Black people, unemployment due to discrimination, and financial stress because "the man" will not hire a Sista or Brotha put a significant strain on Black relationships and communities. Families cannot put food on the table or pay for essential needs. Black parents are often working two or three jobs to make ends meet, and then their children suffer because the parents are not at home or are not emotionally available. This can result in many different scenarios, but the ones I have seen most often when working with children in therapy are the kids turning

to drugs, developing eating disorders, getting involved in unhealthy or non-productive activities, and/or experiencing other mental health issues, such as depression. I am not saying it is the parents' fault. It is a system failure with roots in racism, anti-blackness, and discrimination. So even when we Black folks are doing our best to love on one another, to be good parents, and to provide for our families, the force of toxic whiteness is still relentlessly wreaking havoc in our lives. This is our struggle.

And finally, our struggle includes our personal stuff. Physical health issues, mental health issues, personality problems, unresolved grief, festering anger, relationship heartbreak, trauma, community violence, and just regular ol' personal challenges—they all create struggle, and sometimes they impede our ability to understand, give, and receive love. Life all by itself can be a struggle. Trust issues, failed past relationships, mommy and daddy issues, and low self-esteem create barriers to give and receive love. If you have experienced any of these challenges, I empathize with you, because I have faced many of them too. This is our struggle.

I have been knocked down by family disagreements and relationship issues. My journey to create resolve in my spirit and overcome such challenges has not been easy. Looking back on the pain, I thought I would never survive my moments in the dark valleys. But as I write these words, I realize what got me through those moments was my deep faith in a creator greater than myself, and the beliefs that I deserve to be at peace and to give and receive love. I am love and so are you.

Over the years, I have learned we each have a *deserve level,* and it can increase with consistent and healthy beliefs and actions. The downside is it can *decrease* when we stop prioritizing ourselves, stop putting boundaries in place, and stop holding people accountable for not honoring those boundaries. What's beautiful about this concept is we are each in control of our own deserve level. We get to decide what we deserve. We get to decide who deserves to be in our lives and who gets access to our love. We get to decide how we want to be treated. We get to set the rules and boundaries of our love. We get to decide how others treat us. We get to decide who we allow into our hearts, minds, and spirits.

- Maybe you do not believe you deserve love that is honest, loyal, and authentic. You do.

- Maybe you are settling for the wrong sort of love. You should not.

- Maybe you *are* expecting or demanding the love you deserve. You should.

- Maybe you think there isn't anyone who knows how to love you. There is.

- Maybe you *do* believe you deserve the love you desire. You are right.

- Maybe you are giving and receiving love right now, but you want to learn how to do it better. You can.

- Maybe you have someone who loves you, but you want them to love you better. You can learn how to ask for what you need.

You cannot make anyone love you, but you can set your deserve level high, and you can expect folks—both family and friends—to love you the way you want to be loved. And you should expect your lovers to love you according to your deserve level. What do you deserve? What kind of love do you deserve? If you don't know, how do you expect to receive it? Only you can determine the answers to these questions, and that is a beautiful privilege.

Living and existing in your Black skin is a Beautiful Struggle. The ups and downs. The wins and losses. The joys and sorrows. The pains and pleasures. It is all part of the Beautiful Struggle. You may not be able to control the part of the struggle that occurs outside yourself, but you can choose to control the Beautiful Struggle within yourself. You cannot change the past, nor can you predict or control the future. You can hold folks who have hurt you accountable, and it is YOUR responsibility to do the work to heal your wounds. Your abusers and oppressors are responsible for the harm they cause you, but *you* are responsible for your healing and liberation. So, you can either choose to continue to blame them for your circumstances and stay stuck, or you can choose to create a new way of being, living, and loving. Because you deserve to be loved and to give love. To be love.

You have the right to be angry and sad about how you've been treated in the past. You have the right to feel some kind of way about the suffering and struggle you've endured. Your pain. Your rage. Your anger. Your sadness. It is all justified! And you have the right to not let your anger and sadness consume and engulf you. You have the right to be outraged about your struggle and suffering. And you have the right to release your suffering and allow healing and love to thrive even as

you struggle. It is not either-or, Folks. Love is simple, and it is complex. You can hold yourself and others accountable for the struggle, and you can choose to be loved and to give love. You can acknowledge your pain, and you can heal from it. You can let love revitalize and restore you.

Are you willing to love today? Right now, in this moment? It's time to make a decision. It's time to choose. I hope you choose love that is good for your health. I hope you choose to let love return you to yourself. I hope you let love save you from yourself. Let love heal and nourish you. Let love inspire and please you. Let love allow you to be seen and heard. Let love allow your soul to be nurtured. Let it allow you to be understood, held, and cared for. Love. Sip it slowly; sip it every day. Overindulge in it. Wallow in it as often as you can. Let it be a priority. Your first choice. Believe you deserve to receive love in the way you want it. I hope you set your deserve level as high as possible.

Love is the one thing whiteness cannot take from you. Toxic whiteness has stolen a lot from Black people, including lives, future generations, languages, traditions, and our heritage. Toxic whiteness continues to take and steal from us today. And as you know, where there is no justice, there is no peace. No inner peace nor community peace. The plight of Black people is real, and so is our pain and suffering. The struggle is real. Yet even with the often enormous and overwhelming external struggles we endure, we always have a choice to cultivate a sacred space within to love. What is keeping you from love? Will you, above all else, choose love?

Here is an excerpt from my poem "Black People" (included in the Resources section of this book) that talks about our love choices:

*"Black love is powerful.*

*Black love inspires.*

*Black love heals.*

    *And we get to choose it in every moment.*

    *We get to choose to love ourselves.*

    *We get to choose to love each other.*

    *We get to choose to love our families and our communities.*

*Black love is beautiful; it is you and me.*

*Black love; that's who we be."*

—Catrice M. Jackson

Black love. It is essential. Choose it! Choose love over fear every day. To be and give love is revolutionary. It is the resistance we must exercise to thrive personally and as a community. It is *our* Beautiful Struggle.

## LOVE JUICE

*Love is loving yourself when no one else does. Do it.*

—Catriceology

## LOVE NOTES

What is your struggle, and what is the beauty within it?

_____

_____

_____

_____

_____

How are you using the master's tools against your fellow Black people?

_____

_____

_____

_____

_____

What will you do to raise your deserve level?

_____

_____

_____

_____

_____

**LOVE BOMB**

"Love takes off the masks that we fear we cannot live without and know we cannot live within."

James Baldwin
*The Fire Next Time*

# CHAPTER THREE

# Love Looks Good on You

*"Embark on the journey of LOVE.
It takes you from yourself to yourself."*

**Rumi**

My one word for 2021 is *LOVE*. I did not choose this word; it chose me. Every year I ask God to give me ONE word with which to embody, live out, and manifest my desires and God's purpose for me. A couple of months before I went on sabbatical in September 2020, variations on the word "love" kept dropping into my spirit. Words like "compassion," "passion," and "affection." I also kept seeing and hearing the number nine. You may not believe in astrology, divine coincidence, or synchronicity, but I believe there is meaning in it all. According to astrology, the number nine represents completeness, universal spiritual laws, divine faith, and love. The number nine is said to be the strongest and most powerful of all the numbers, and it is humanitarian and compassionate. Some folks even speculate that the number nine is magic! When I synthesize the words "completeness," "passion," "affection," "strong," "powerful," "humanitarian," and "compassion," the one and best word that comes to mind is "love." Love is magic, and to love and be loved is magical!

I believe we can create magic even as we struggle with love, which is what makes Black love a Beautiful Struggle. Black people have proven

this truth for generations while enduring unimaginable pain, strife, and struggle. There is no other group of people more resourceful, creative, and innovative than Black folks. I am grateful for my ancestors—the ones gone long ago, and the ones who have passed on in the last twenty years or so. I don't have to look back too far to see the magic of Black love in motion. My maternal grandmother passed away in 2010, and I miss her dearly. I learned so much from her vicariously, simply by being in her presence. She had a hack and remedy for just about everything. I have adopted many of her innovative ideas into my own life. My Gran was a resilient and resourceful problem solver. And so is my mother.

My mother was cash-poor much of her life due to being disabled. Shortly after having me, she suffered a back injury at work and had to have spinal surgery, which resulted in her not being able to work a job. But she worked hard as a single mother raising two children on a fixed income. We may have not had much money, but we were rich in love, and she created a living space that was more extravagant than those of some of my wealthier friends. She was a master seamstress and creator. A creative genius, to be honest.

Although we lived a comfortable life despite not having much money, I watched my mother ride an emotional rollercoaster because of financial stress. Sometimes her resourcefulness was just not enough to make ends meet. I hated watching her "scuffle to scratch and survive," as she called it. Despite the struggle, we lived and loved the best we knew how. It was a Beautiful Struggle. My grandmother and mother created magic in the face of chaos and challenges. And no matter what was going on around them, they always chose love.

Unfortunately, my grandmother and mother did not always choose themselves first. They did not prioritize their self-care and self-love. Instead, they poured all their love into their children, grandchildren, the community, and other folks who needed support. It is a choice they made for their own reasons. I suspect it was not only what Black women did naturally, but also what was expected of them by their generation. They were conditioned by their mothers, and their mothers were conditioned by *their* mothers. And as you can imagine, the generations before them had no choice but to work their fingers to the bone while sacrificing their own joy, pleasure, and self-care. Their sacrifice is the reason I am here. Because of them, I can. And because of them, I can make different choices, and I have. I will.

The way our parents and grandparents expressed love may have allowed them to survive, but they did not necessarily thrive. Or at least, they didn't thrive in the sense of being in love with themselves and receiving the love they deserved. One thing is for sure after witnessing my mother's and grandmother's Beautiful Struggles: I knew I wanted and deserved more for me and my future children. I was not sure how I was going to love myself and show love to my children, but I knew I had to do some things differently. I knew I could not repeat the bitterness of my mother's and grandmother's Beautiful Struggle. Deep down inside, I knew I deserved better and more. What about you? Are you settling in love? Do you know what you deserve? Do you need to unlearn and release the bitterness in your parents' and grandparents' Beautiful Struggles?

The ability to *believe* you deserve is a mental muscle that must be strengthened every day. An old colleague introduced me to the concept of each of us having a *deserve level*, which I first talked about in the previous chapter. My interpretation of her teachings is that your deserve level is like an invisible line in your mind. This line determines how much goodness and splendor you will allow yourself to have. This invisible psychological line also determines how much you will put up with or settle for. Is your deserve level high or low?

I wrote about the deserve level in my book *Unleash Your Significance: Activate the Audacity to Be All You Are Destined to Be.* Chapter 6 of that book contains a quick and easy checklist to determine how high or low your deserve level is; I've included it here for your convenience:

Put a checkmark by the statements that *most often* apply to your life:

_____ I feel more overwhelmed than I feel in control.

_____ I experience more worry or doubt than I feel confidence.

_____ I feel heavy and bogged down more than I feel energized.

_____ I feel overworked and undercompensated.

_____ I feel stuck more than I feel like I am moving forward.

_____ I feel unappreciated often by those I love.

_____ I often think I could have a better job or bring more money into my business.

_____ I feel awkward or uncomfortable when people give me gifts or compliments.

_____ I often attract negative or toxic people in my life.

_____ I frequently wonder when it is going to be my turn.

_____ I know I am in situations that do not feel good, but I don't take the steps to free myself.

_____ I often say or think, "something is better than nothing."

_____ I often envy other people's successes, relationships, careers, or finances.

_____ I feel like I am settling in more than one area of my life.

—Catrice M. Jackson, *Unleash Your Significance*

The more checkmarks you have, the lower your deserve level is. You have either allowed the invisible psychological line in your head to be drawn by others, or you have drawn it low yourself. That invisible line indicates what you believe you deserve. Of course, the checklist is not conclusive, but it does offer enough information to give you some insight into your beliefs about what you do and don't deserve.

This is where you get to choose self-love:

1. Pause and write the answers to these two questions:
   - *Why am I carrying this emotional weight?*
   - *Am I actively choosing to carry it, and if so, why?*

2. Now go back and put a star by the statements in the checklist you have *partial* control over.

3. Finally, underline the statements you have *complete* control over.

What did you discover in answering the two questions? Are you worrying and feeling overwhelmed? Do you feel bogged down, stuck, and unappreciated? Do you have more energy-draining, toxic people in your life than you desire? Do you tend to have envious thoughts and feelings of jealousy? Are you settling, or are you setting boundaries for yourself? If this is generally how you are feeling, does it feel loving?

As for being in partial or complete control, I realize some of the checklist's statements involve external factors that may be out of your control, but most of them do not. You can either do something to change those external factors, or you can accept them. For example, I know racism and global anti-blackness are external threats to my ability to experience peace. But instead of just complaining about them, I do something every day to combat them and establish justice for Black people. I may not win or succeed every day, but I do not just accept these threats and do nothing about them. I am also aware that I may not see the end of racism in my lifetime, but I will fight for justice until I take my last breath, just like my ancestors did. Will *you* accept the external factors, or will you do something about them so you can fully give and receive love, and experience greater peace and pleasure?

I also realize there are many other factors at play here. For example, maybe you are dealing with your mental health status, your financial situation, or whether you have an effective support system Those factors are real and valid, but again, what can you control? What are you in control of? To raise your deserve level, you must choose to do something about the circumstances for which you have partial or complete control. Otherwise, you will keep yourself in a space of settling for whatever.

Remember: you are significant. You matter, and you are worthy of whatever you desire. You are worthy of peace, and you deserve to love yourself, to be loved, and to give love. Let's dive a bit deeper into the deserve level and what it is. The good news is your deserve level is not fixed. You have the power to raise it if you choose. Here is another excerpt from Chapter 6 of my book *Unleash Your Significance*, which defines the term "deserve level" and includes some strategies on how to raise it:

> Your deserve level is a combination of the internal images you have of yourself, your self-esteem, what you believe to be true about you, and a culmination of the internal messages (beliefs) you have about yourself based on other people's opinions. This psycho-emotional concoction draws the deserve line in your mind, and, until you intentionally do the mental work to raise the line, you'll feel unworthy of what you really deserve. You can start now. Change will not happen overnight, but, with daily practice, you WILL raise your deserve level. And, until you raise it, you will continue to settle, and it will be difficult for you to create your *"more"* and enjoy it.
>
> ### TIPS TO RAISE YOUR DESERVE LEVEL
>
> - **Ask for help.** I suggest a licensed therapist or a mindset coach. Whomever you choose, they need to be someone objective who not only *sees, honors, and celebrates* your significance but can help YOU see, honor, and celebrate it. Be willing to be vulnerable. It is in vulnerability that you become humble, healed, and happy.

- **Start forgiving and begin with you.** Holding grudges keeps you in captivity. Ever notice how the people you haven't forgiven are moving forward with and enjoying their lives? The only one brooding, harboring, and feeling miserable is you. Forgiveness is a beautiful gift. Set you and others free. You can practice daily affirmations that start with *"I now forgive myself {or the other person} for _____. I release it completely, and I am free and happy."* Do this as many times as necessary until you no longer hold a grudge.

- **Celebrate others.** It's easy to envy and be jealous of the success and possessions of others and it's pretty normal. When you see someone being, doing, or having what you desire, pause and celebrate them. Feel the excitement with them and know that if they can be, do, or have it, so can you. ENERGY is everything. The more positive energy you put out into the world the more positivity you'll experience. **Don't think you are jealous or envious of others? Next time someone shares great news or gets something new, notice how you FEEL. If you don't feel LOVE feelings… you are jealous or envious.**

- **Practice gratitude.** When you see your friends, family, and colleagues living or experiencing *their* more… be grateful for what you have. There are plenty of people in the world who wish they were you and/or have what you have. Being grateful and expressing gratitude opens the doors for you to receive *your* more.

- **Stop wishing and start doing your work.** If you don't get in the game, you'll never know if you can win. Don't be afraid to fail. Failure is part of the journey. Expect it because along the way it will happen. Failure is not losing. Failure is feedback that tells you to try something else and try again. When you fail, instead of thinking and saying things like, *"I suck. I'm no good. I'm never doing that again,"* say *"I learned what did not work,"* or *"I learned how to do it better."*

- **Decide what you want.** Make a list of what you really want. Believe you deserve it all. Set some achievable yet flexible goals. Determine what you need and who you need to help you achieve the goals. Create a plan and get to work. Nothing works if you don't work it. If you're not seeing progress, check your beliefs and raise your deserve level. If you're not advancing forward, get advice from the people you asked to help you. If you're not yet experiencing your more, reassess your strategy and change it or add a different approach to the plan. No matter what, don't quit! Be curious. Explore alternatives and other options. Be sure to celebrate *every* forward movement and success.

- **Unleashing your significance and living a life that matters must have meaning.** Are you living a meaningful life? What does meaning mean to you? By nature, we are selfish, self-serving human beings. We are wired to survive or die. It is in the relentless quest to survive that we often fail to appreciate who we are and how far we've come. I'm a naturally driven person, so the pursuit of success is in my genes. Once I set a goal, I usually do not need external motivation to accomplish it, unless of course, the goal is related to weight loss; then I could certainly use my own cheerleading squad. I'm working on it (smile).

—Catrice M. Jackson, *Unleash Your Significance*

Love is simple and complex. Loving yourself takes dedication and work. Perhaps it is time to embark on a journey to return *yourself to yourself*, as Rumi advised. Don't make the same mistakes as Dorothy in the movie *The Wiz*. You don't have to go on a fantastic voyage and hook up with the Scarecrow, the Tin Man, and the Cowardly Lion to ease on down your Yellow Brick Road. You do not need the Munchkins or Glinda, the Good Witch of the South. And as far as the Wiz goes, you do not need a grand wizard to work magic in your life. The journey to find yourself and love yourself is not an *external* journey. It is within you.

It is time to return home. All you need is to say yes to embarking on a journey to go home to yourself. And once you get there, look around at your mess and clean it up. Put things in order. Organize your mental space. Clean out your soul closet. Get rid of what you do not want or need. Make space for new and beautiful things. And once you get your inner space cleaned up, do not let people run through your house with their dirty shoes on (their negativity and toxic vibes). Demand they take their shoes off at the door (set rules for how people treat you). And remind them how to behave (set emotional boundaries and expectations) in YOUR house (in YOUR life). This is what self-love looks like.

Love. It can and does look good on you. What do I mean by that? Well, when you are loving at full capacity and love is pouring into your soul cup, you glow. You sparkle and shine. You feel light and liberated. You feel a sense of freedom. You walk a deliberate walk. You speak affirmation and celebration. Love looks good on you!

When you give and receive love, it is good for your health. You prioritize yourself. You set boundaries, and you protect your emotional and spiritual energy. When love looks good on you, your attitude is more optimistic and confident. Love looking good on you creates space for understanding, compassion, and empathy. When love looks good on you, you don't take no wooden nickels, as my Gran used to say, aka you don't let people take advantage of you. Love looks good on you! It feels good too.

Most times, love is light. Love allows you to relax, be, and breathe. There is gratitude, peace, and joy in love. The euphoria of loving and being loved is priceless. What a gift it is to love and be loved! The gift that begins with you loving yourself, whatever that looks like for you. Maybe your idea of self-love is not anything I have described so far. No problem. You get to choose what loving yourself, and what giving and receiving love, look and feel like for you. How will you make love look good on you?

Perhaps when you completed the checklist earlier in this chapter, you didn't check off *any* of the statements. If so, good for you! If you were honest with yourself when you did the exercise and got that result, I would speculate your deserve level is high. And guess what? There is fluidity in your deserve level, so you can take yours higher if you choose. This fluidity also means your deserve level may decrease when certain circumstances arise. For example, it could be high, and then infidelity happens in your relationship, or a friend betrays you, or perhaps a family member turns their back on you. Even your own personal physical and mental health challenges can make your deserve level fluctuate. All these situations—and so many others!—can take you away from home. They can stagnate your self-love journey. If that happens, I encourage you to revisit the advice and strategies described in this book.

As with other love journeys, the journey of self-love is not a race, nor is it a sprint. It is a marathon, and sometimes the path is rugged and lonely. But always know this: it is *you* who will return yourself to yourself. It is *you* who has the power to go home again as many times as you need to. It is *you* who must be in control of your love journey. Love yourself even when others don't. Make love look good on you!

## LOVE JUICE

*Love is teaching people how to love you and releasing them with love when they don't want to learn.*

—*Catriceology*

## LOVE NOTES

What do you deserve? Elaborate, and be clear.

_____

_____

_____

_____

_____

What do you need to do and be for yourself on your love journey?

_____

_____

_____

_____

_____

What do you need to do to return to yourself and go home?

_____

_____

_____

_____

_____

**LOVE BOMB**

"You've got to learn
to leave the table when love's
no longer being served."

Nina Simone
*"You've Got to Learn"*

# CHAPTER FOUR

# Above All Else... Love

*"We are here to do two things: to love and
to be of service to others."*

Catrice M. Jackson

You are not here by accident or coincidence. On the contrary, you are a miracle in motion and here for a purpose. And I believe you are here for a special destiny designed uniquely for you, and only for you. Maybe you know what your purpose is, and maybe you have no idea at all. I do not know what your spiritual practice or belief is; however, I believe in a power greater than humankind, and I refer to this power either as my creator, Spirit, and/or God. I believe the creator allowed you to be here in your physical body for a reason. Many people like to complicate the meaning of the word "purpose." Here is a powerful quote about purpose from John P. Schuster's book *Answering Your Call: A Guide for Living Your Deepest Purpose:*

> "God gives us the brief before our birth before our soul's descent into flesh. But after our births we remember the briefing only dimly, because taking on a body weakens the ability of the spirit to remember who we are and what we are here for. –So, the nagging sense of having forgotten something important, the longing without cause, the calls that haunt us like whispers from

a little too far away, come from our remembering parts and fragments of the briefing. The calling is not forgotten entirely, but is muted and fuzzy, like a distant radio station whose signal is filled with static."

— Doris Lessing, as quoted by John P. Schuster in *Answering Your Call*

I will not spend much time talking about purpose except as it pertains to love. You can delve into my perspectives about purpose in Chapter 2 of my book *Unleash Your Significance*. Here is an excerpt from that chapter introducing my thoughts on the subject:

"Your purpose is NOT a mystery. It's not a figment of your imagination. It's not this made-up thing that you'll never find, and it's not only for 'special' people. Every person has a purpose, or they would not be here. Either you can reconnect with spirit and get back in alignment with your pre-determined purpose or you can continue to exercise your own free will and do it your way. Many times when you do it your way, you never find the path to your purpose.

"Let's consider the possibility that what Doris Lessing says is true (and I believe it is); the first key to discovering your purpose is to *remember* who you are. She talked about the body weakening the ability of the spirit to remember. That means the spirit, your creator, *has the answer.* Thus, the further away from spirit (God), and the more we are in our body (consumed with the natural state of our being), the less we remember about our purpose, our unique assignment in the world, our significance.

"If you are still searching for your purpose, start by reconnecting to your source, your spirit, and your creator. Your purpose is already within you; you just have to remember it. You remember by canceling out any and all definitions, labels, and titles you've allowed the world (and you) to put on you. You remember by re-defining who you really are and declaring your bodacious I AM. You remember who you are by choosing to not allow others to victimize you and that includes yourself. You remember by decreasing the static of the outside world and tuning into the frequency of who you desire to be and who your creator says you are. You remember by intentionally listening to the whispers of your soul and nudges of your intuition. All the answers you seek are there. Make the choice today to go inward to get and receive them."

—Catrice M. Jackson, *Unleash Your Significance*

Maybe you do not believe in God or Spirit, or maybe you are agnostic. Regardless of what or who you believe in, you are here for a special reason. Regarding purpose, I believe it is quite simple. We are here to love and to serve. After all, what else is there to do? And by "love," I mean to love yourself first and fill your own cup with self-love, and then you can serve love to others from your overflow. That's right! We should not be serving love to people directly from our cups, but instead be so filled with love that it abundantly overflows and spills into the lives of others. Let's keep it real. If you let folks suck the love out of you, they will. They will take advantage of you; they will use and abuse you. They will take you for granted, lie to you, cheat on you, hit you, and treat you like a disposable resource instead of valuing and appreciating you. If any of these things happen, your love source will be depleted unless you've kept your love cup full. So, above all else… love you. Fill your cup every day.

The American Public Health Association (APHA) estimates that one in four women have abortions in their lifetime (Jones and Jerman, 2017). I share this statistic to show that a lot of abortions occur in a year, along with many stillbirths and miscarriages. So, when a woman carries a baby full term, it is a miracle. And if you are reading this book, *you* are a miracle. This is not to say that those who were not born are not valuable and special. It's to say that based on these statistics and all the possible complications that can happen during pregnancy and childbirth… you survived them, and you are here! Because you beat the odds, I believe you are here for a special reason, a purpose. And at the fundamental level, that purpose is to be of service to others.

Simply put, "to be of service" means to serve or give to others with no expectation of reciprocity. "To be of service" can also mean serving others with your gifts and talents. And while having *no expectation of reciprocity* is noble, you can also be of service and get compensated for your time and energy. It just depends on your perspectives on being of service and how a particular service aligns with your values. Giving and serving from your heart is an act of love that you exist to do. Take a minute and revel in the miracle of you!

If you give and receive love while being of service to others, you are fundamentally living out your existence's purpose. There is so much more than these basics, though. Remember what I said in Chapter 1 of this book? It is so vital that it is worth repeating:

Love is wondrous and splendid! Love is attraction and fondness. Love is exhilarating and consuming. Love is respect, affinity, and passion. Love is patience and tenderness. Love is compassion, understanding, and kindness. Love is erotic, sensual, and sexual. Love is empathy, trust, and honesty. Love is complicated and intricate. Love is simple and pure. Love can be rare, priceless, and altruistic.

There are not enough words to describe love, and the great news is we get to define it as we choose. We get to give it and receive it as we choose. Here are some things I know for sure:

- Love governs the way we think and feel about ourselves and others.
- Love determines how we perceive, engage with, and treat ourselves and others.
- Love allows us to be seen and heard.
- Love allows us to be held, understood, and cared for.
- Love is healing.
- Love is nourishment.
- Love is food for the soul.

The fact that we get to experience this celestial brew of emotions is astounding! Imagine being able to sip this concoction every single day. Imagine feeling the splendor in giving and receiving love, and in being of service with love. You can do all these things if you choose.

The best way to be of service to others is to first be of service to yourself. An empty cup cannot produce an overflow with which to serve others. Prioritizing YOUR care, nourishment, needs, and desires

is part of the self-love journey. You do not have to be anyone's mule, emotional punching bag, or disposable resource. I want to share some of my personal love declarations with you, and I hope they inspire you to create your own:

- Love is recognizing habits that don't serve you and changing them.

- Love is learning the triggers that cause you to spiral down and replacing them with motivators to rise.

- Love is making daily choices that serve your highest good.

- Love is learning what takes from your vitality and ceasing to engage in those draining activities and transactions.

- Love is taking responsibility for who you want to be and how you want to live.

- Love is generosity. Love is reciprocity.

- Love is an open hand, not a closed fist.

- Teaching people how to love you is an act of self-love. If they truly love you, they will adjust.

- Love is rooted in action. Put your love in motion.

- Love is knowing who treats you like an option and taking the option away from them.

- Love is refusing to shrink to keep folks comfortable.

- Love is refusing to hide your happiness and joy.

- Love is expressing your full range of emotions regardless of what others think.

- Love is not hiding your blessings, your joy, or your happiness, because you know others need to see that those feelings are possible for them too.

- Love is being with people who are good for your health.

- Love is choosing the kind of life you want and saying NO to anything that does not nourish you.

- Love is refusing to tolerate folks who celebrate you behind closed doors, but not in public.

- Love is openly celebrating who you love while they are alive, including giving them their flowers now.

- Love is releasing people who are connected to you only so they can take from you, spy on you, and hate on you. Let them go!

- When you know who the takers are and still allow them to access your magic, that ain't self-love, it's self-sabotage. Release them!

- Love is paying attention to whose energy changes when you set boundaries.

- Love is you versus you. There is no competition, and you will win.

- Love is speaking your truth even if you are afraid, and even if doing so does not bring resolution.

- Love is knowing that refusing to express your feelings can make you sick, and choosing to not be sick.

- Love is demanding reciprocity for your love and walking away when you don't get it.

These statements exemplify self-love in action. This kind of self-love takes courage. Courage to believe you deserve love and respect. Courage to declare and set your love boundaries. And courage to hold people accountable for how they love you.

How did you feel when you read these declarations? Did your heart expand or contract? Did the declarations inspire you or make you feel uncomfortable? I hope you paid attention to how you felt, because there is a message for you in your reaction. If you did not feel affirmed or inspired by these declarations, then subconsciously you may be afraid to demand the love you deserve. It may also indicate that your deserve level is low. And if this is the case, you should go back and re-read Chapter 3. Perhaps you are worried about getting pushback or afraid that people will misunderstand you and walk away. Well, here is the truth: it takes a lot of self-love and courage to declare and demand how you want to be loved, and to be willing to have your demands misunderstood.

A hard truth is that some people in your life are not really FOR you. Most people are WITH you for what they can get, take, and steal from you. I have come to realize this truth over the years, and it is a hard pill to swallow, especially when you love and are *for* someone who is only *with* you. Unfortunately, we must learn the hard way about some folks. And once God spoke to me and told me to make love my focus for this year, I began to clearly see who is for me versus who is with me.

Another truth is that we already know who these people are, the ones who are with us for selfish reasons. We see the signs. We hear the whispers. The emotional nudges are telling us all the time, but we choose to ignore those hints because we want to see the best in folks.

Unfortunately, when we don't listen to our intuition, our gut, and our wise mind, we end up being let down and hurt.

I am mastering the skill of discernment with each day that passes. As an intuitive person and empath, I am already tuned into people's feelings and behaviors. And now that I am on my love journey, my ability to see the truth through the bullshit is laser sharp. Some people have referred to me as a human lie detector, and they are right. Often, I am a mirror that folks do not want to look into. One thing is for sure: I see through words and behaviors that are not aligned with the truth.

Let me share some insights I have gleaned over the years. Love for me is two things:

- Teaching others how to love me (aka how to respect and engage with me)
- Learning how to love myself better

Remember: if folks love you, they will be willing to learn how to honor, respect, and engage with you in the way you desire. If they are not willing, they don't truly love you. And it is up to you whether or not you accept their unwillingness to love you the way you want them to. Another truth is that those who love you will celebrate your wins as if those wins were their own. It's hard to clap when you've got one hand behind your back, right? People who claim they love you but who do not clap when you win are suspect. Pay attention to that kind of behavior. Those people with one hand behind their backs are concealing ulterior motives and hater thoughts.

Loving yourself requires you to walk away when love is not present, to celebrate your damn self, and to keep on shining! People who do not clap when you win are not your people. Those folks are usually with you, not for you. People who think you shine too much are not your people. It's time for you to stop holding back your joy, accomplishments, and success. You are a lighthouse, and somebody is seeking your light. If you don't shine, how will they find you? When people tell you that you shine too much and/or you should not celebrate your shine, then trust me, they do not really love you. Do not waste your precious life source on worrying about what other people think of your shine. Do not be afraid to honor and celebrate *yourself!* Above all else… love you! Love yourself enough to never dim your light.

Love yourself enough to completely trust your intuition. The whisper. The gut feeling. The nudge in your heart. The discomfort in your belly. The divine wisdom that comes from knowing thyself. We often regret NOT listening to our wise inner self. Trust that energy you feel. Trust the vibes you get. Trust all those messages you receive that disturb your spirit in some way. One of the biggest betrayals is the betrayal of self. Like my mama taught me, *"All that glitters is not gold."* People are often not who they say they are, and when their words do not match their behaviors, trust that shit! James Baldwin is right when he said, *"I can't believe what you say, because I see what you do."* Let folks' behavior be what you need to see so you can do what you need to do. And once someone shows you who they are, believe them and act accordingly.

And here is a final truth: once someone shows you what role you play in *their* life, play it, or leave the set. You do not have to be a prop in anyone's story, because you are the star of your own story. Takers, users, and abusers love folks who do not love themselves enough to

set boundaries. Set them anyway for your self-love. You will know who the takers are because they will go silent or get angry when you start setting boundaries for yourself. Or they will say, *"You've changed."* Yes, you have changed! You are exercising the courage to fully love yourself and to set boundaries and expectations for how you will be loved. Folks who also embody self-love, and those who love and respect you, will celebrate and honor your boundaries. Love is choosing people who choose you every day, not just when they need something from you. Those are the takers.

Being on this love journey will require you to let some folks go. I call it "releasing them with love." And I do it often and whenever necessary. It is one of the best ways to show love to myself. It is not always easy, but after I release someone, there is also a release of anxiety and worry. I feel lighter, clearer, and more grounded. The process is bittersweet. Each time I release someone with love, it makes it easier to do it the next time. When you release people with love, it may mean loving them from a distance. With no grudges. You bear them no ill will—in fact, you wish them well. You do not seek revenge. You just let them go while trusting you did the right thing to keep peace in your life and love in your heart. When you release people with love, you preserve your time, love, and energy for the people who consistently show up for you and who love you the way you deserve.

This is an act of radical self-love! Radical self-love is not applauded like the rainbows-and-sprinkles kind of love, because most folks are scared to radically love themselves. Welp, I am not! And when truth is spoken about radical self-love, the afraid go silent. I choose to

be a choir of one, singing in the key of love, no matter who chooses to hear my song.

For me, there is a difference between something being done versus finished. When a situation is *done*, there remains a possibility that it will be resumed. When a situation is *finished*, there is NO possibility of it being resumed, aka its ending is permanently final. Love is knowing what the difference between done versus finished is for you. Love is knowing the difference between *ending a chapter* versus *closing the book*. I've learned from years of providing mental health therapy to a variety of folks that it's always *people* who have caused or are causing pain and struggle for others. Rarely do objects or spaces cause these types of problems. Which means people are hurting people. And before you can heal, move on, and evolve, most times you've got to either accept those people for who they are, or choose to let them go and keep moving. In other words, you shut the book and put it on the shelf forever, and/or you realize you are finished with those people. Love yourself enough to close the book and be finished. Above all else… love you!

Love is reciprocity. When you love folks, you will do your best to *be* to them who they are to you. When you love folks, you will do your best to *do* for them how they do for you. When you love folks, you will do your best to *prioritize* them in the same way they prioritize you. Reciprocity is a universal law of energy. Give and take. Offer and receive. If a relationship is not reciprocal, I do not want it. I hope you say no to those kinds of relationships too. Relationships that are not reciprocal will smother your light. They will have you second-guessing yourself and hiding your brilliance.

Do not dilute yourself or dim your light to make others comfortable. Do not minimize your greatness in front of those who have yet to figure out what their greatness is. We draw people to us by our light. If you are not shining, your people won't be able to find you, and they must find you, because you and your purpose are what they need. This time of crisis and darkness is when you must shine, because a lot of people are hurting and seeking help. Be light. Shine bright. Consistently show up and shine on! One of my favorite Catriceology® quotes is, *"When people cannot handle your light, it is because they have not yet discovered their own, and you are a reminder of that. Do not take it personally and do not shrink or hide. Either they will choose to SHINE, or they will grab a pair of shades."*

If you are on a self-love journey, and/or if you are working to set boundaries and you expect them to be respected, you are in for some revelations you cannot even imagine. Expect silence and ghosting. Expect anger and frustration. Expect folks to walk away. It is like mining for gold. You've got to keep sifting the rocks (those *with* you) so you can find the gold (those *for* you). And when you find that gold, you will be left with priceless and authentic relationships. Relationships where love is reciprocated.

Finally, it is hard to be happy for other people when you subconsciously do not think you deserve what other people have or the wins they experience. Just know that when people are not feeling your shine or are not happy for you, this is what is in their minds. You cannot be worried about it, though. Just keep loving yourself and shining. Hopefully, you will inspire them to do the same.

You may not feel like you deserve much right now, or perhaps you do and want to raise your deserve level. As I said in the previous chapter:

> This fluidity also means your deserve level may decrease when certain circumstances arise. For example, it could be high, and then infidelity happens in your relationship, or a friend betrays you, or perhaps a family member turns their back on you. Even your own personal physical and mental health challenges can make your deserve level fluctuate. All these situations—and so many others!—can take you away from home. They can stagnate your self-love journey. ...
>
> As with other love journeys, the journey of self-love is not a race, nor is it a sprint. It is a marathon, and sometimes the path is rugged. But always know this: it is *you* who will return yourself to yourself. It is *you* who has the power to go home again as many times as you need to. It is *you* who must be in control of your love journey.

Your love journey can be lonely. You will be attacked and misunderstood. You may even lose your way or feel like you want to give up. Do not quit. Do not give up on yourself. You deserve it! Above all else... love you.

Love yourself enough to set boundaries and watch your real friends rise to the top. All others will fall off, disappear, and disconnect from you. When folks go silent after you set boundaries, just know that they were the ones disrespecting you and your boundaries. Maybe

you haven't discovered your life's purpose yet, but know you are here to love and to serve. And before you can love and serve others, you must start with loving and being of service to yourself. One thing I can tell you without a doubt: you must serve people from your overflow, which means you must make sure your cup of self-love is consistently abundant.

You deserve to love yourself and to be loved the way you desire and deserve. Raise your deserve level so you can fully live out your purpose for yourself and for others. This is part of the revolution for justice. Justice is love, and to effectively fight for justice, we must first embody self-love so we can love others enough to fight for their justice, freedom, and liberation. It will be our love for one another that sustains us and propels the movement forward. It will be love that returns us to ourselves. The revolution is and will be love.

Above all else… love. You.

## LOVE JUICE

*Love is justice, and justice is love.*

—*Catriceology*

## LOVE NOTES

How do you plan to love and serve yourself and others?

_____

_____

_____

_____

_____

What and who do you need to release to create a sacred space to love yourself more?

_____

_____

_____

_____

_____

When love looks good on you, what will it look and feel like?

_____

_____

_____

_____

_____

**LOVE BOMB**

"In order to rise from
its own ashes, a Phoenix
first must burn."

Octavia Butler
*Parable of the Talents*

# CHAPTER FIVE

# The Revolution Will Be Love

*"If you don't love the people, sooner or later
you're going to betray the people."*

**Nehanda Isoke Abiodun**

Black people are fighting so many silent and debilitating battles, and we are also tackling the glaring and grotesque injustices happening to and within the global Black community. Black people's daily lives are often daunting and depressing due to extreme amounts of external, global forces that strategically work to destroy our minds, spirits, and bodies. As the world moves into the second year of the global COVID-19 pandemic that is relentlessly ravaging lives, Black people continue to fight systemic and systematic white terrorism and anti-blackness, which are far more diabolical and deadly than any virus.

When COVID-19 hit America in March 2020, I thought, *"Black folks cannot take another lethal hit from anything else. Especially coupled with the horrendous racism in the healthcare industry."* As I discussed in Chapter 2, Black people are already misdiagnosed, prescribed the wrong treatments, and discriminated against in healthcare systems across the country. Poor Black folks are treated with even greater indignities. Flash forward to May 2020. While the world was on house arrest (aka stuck in their homes) due to the pandemic, a Black man named George Floyd was mercilessly lynched on camera for the whole world to see with zero shame.

There has been nothing positive about the COVID-19 pandemic, and I feel terrible about all the lives lost due to the virus. May those who have passed away rest in peace, and may their families be comforted and healed from the grief of loss. During the summer of 2020, people all over the world had to—for the first time, and with undistracted eyes due to being locked down—see the injustice of George Floyd being sadistically murdered. Media outlets provided extensive coverage of his murder by asphyxiation due to a white police officer kneeling on his neck for eight minutes and forty-six seconds. A Minneapolis police officer named Derek Chauvin strangled George Floyd to death in front of everyone at the crime scene, including his fellow officers, aka his partners in crime. While thousands of people in America were dying from the COVID-19 virus, George Floyd died from the virus of white terrorism. Had we not been in lockdown, he would have been just another Black man who allegedly did not comply with the police—just another Black man murdered by the police in a "Black man said, police said" situation.

If there was any smidge of light during this pandemic, it was this moment of truth that revealed how the police in America have been going unpunished for killing unarmed Black people (Black people in general). Finally! And hopefully, people can now see the violence being perpetrated against Black people by the police for what it is: anti-black, state-sanctioned white terrorism. Unfortunately, not everyone will see it this way, but most Black folks already know this truth. After all, they have been living it since 1619. And white folks have been lynching us since 1619 too.

For the first time in U.S. history, I believe some Americans' eyes were opened, and they saw the horrendous crimes that have been committed against Black bodies for centuries. Derek Chauvin's murder of George Floyd was a gruesome display of the lack of empathy for Black bodies. Many white folks feel these injustices, but it has been rare for them to act on them. And although it was not a bloody murder, it was even more sinister than bullets in the back, because Derek Chauvin casually kneeled on a Black man's body knowing damn well he was being filmed. He did not care. He knew he was being filmed, and he continued to lynch a man with no regard for that man's life.

Why? Because he could, and because he believed he would not be punished and held accountable for his sadistic murder. Why? Because throughout our history, police officers all over the country have been getting away with murder. They are not being convicted for murdering Black people at the rate they should be. Why? Because at one time it was legal to lynch Black folks. And let's be honest: policing in the U.S. as we know it today originated in the slave patrols created to catch and punish runaway enslaved Africans.

Here is an excerpt from a National Law Enforcement Museum blog post describing the relationship between slave patrols and this country's early police forces:

> "Organized policing was one of the many types of social controls imposed on enslaved African Americans in the South. Physical and psychological violence took many forms, including an overseer's brutal whip, the intentional breakup of families, deprivation of food and other necessities, and the private employment of slave catchers to track down runaways. ...

"First formed in 1704 in South Carolina, patrols lasted over 150 years, only technically ending with the abolition of slavery during the Civil War. However, just because the patrols lost their lawful status did not mean that their influence died out in 1865. Hadden argues there are distinct parallels between the legal slave patrols before the war and extralegal terrorization tactics used by vigilante groups during Reconstruction, most notoriously, the Ku Klux Klan.

"After the Civil War, Southern police departments often carried over aspects of the patrols. These included systematic surveillance, the enforcement of curfews, and even notions of who could become a police officer. Though a small number of African Americans joined the police force in the South during Reconstruction, they met active resistance.

"Though law enforcement looks very different today, the profession developed from practices implemented in the colonies."

— Chelsea Hansen, "Slave Patrols: An Early Form of American Policing," National Law Enforcement Museum's Blog: *On the Beat*, July 10, 2019

There you have it, Folks! Just in case you didn't know this history, now you do. The "police" have been terrorizing Black people ever since we were brought to this continent to be bought and sold as "property." And we have been persisting, fighting, resisting, and trying to survive this terrorism ever since too. The Movement for Black Lives is as old as the first slave ship that arrived in 1619. We have been fighting

for freedom and liberation for a long, tiring time—to no avail. Four hundred years later, and not much has changed for us. There is an illusion of inclusion and justice for all, but we know the illusion is far from the truth.

How are we still even here? How do we keep surviving this treachery century after century? Is there something within our psyche or our DNA that allows us to survive—and for some of us, thrive—in the face of daily white terrorism? I am not sure, and I have not done any formal research on this phenomenon, but one word comes to mind as a compelling reason: love. Since day one, white people and NBPOC have not loved Black people. Unfortunately, some Black folks do not love Black people either. So, it must be the Black people who *do* love Black people who have been keeping us alive and surviving for generations. The most powerful force in the universe. Love! Love has sustained us. The revolution will be (and must be) love!

I am grateful for all the Black folks who loved the Black folks who came before me, and I am grateful for all the Black folks who continue to love each other today. Kinship (Community) Love is what has kept us alive and striving for justice, freedom, and liberation. The love derived from our rich roots, connectedness, culture, heritage, and communal family has fortified our fight for justice. The affinity we share with Mother Africa and our common ancestry has strengthened us so we can fight for survival. Our Kinship Love allows us to empathize with other Black people in the struggle for liberation. We have an uncanny ability to love other Black people even when we dislike or disagree with them, because outside of a few real allies here and there, we're all we've got! Some of us say, "*We all we got*" and do not really mean it, but I believe

most of us do. And it is true. Without Black people loving, supporting, and advocating for Black people, where would we be? Kinship Love is so powerful and instrumental to our survival and ability to thrive that it is worth repeating its characteristics from Chapter 1:

- *Compassion:* To have deep feelings of tenderness, sympathy, and understanding of someone else's struggle or pain with a desire to alleviate their pain.

- *Affinity:* To have an organic liking for someone who shares your interests and/or desires.

- *Connectedness:* To be linked with another person on a soul level, anchored in shared ancestry.

- *Solidarity:* To be in alliance with someone who shares a common struggle or goal.

- *Acceptance:* To receive and honor others as they are.

- *Empathy:* To sense, understand, and share someone else's feelings.

- *Altruism:* To be genuinely concerned for other people's welfare without ulterior motives, often at the risk of self.

The global fight for Black liberation will not be won without love. The fight especially requires Kinship Love. We will not win without it. We will not evolve without love, and we will not be free and liberated without love. Kinship Love. Black liberation has stagnated and been delayed because we cannot seem to unify and/or organize with one accord. There are many other reasons for this, including our own physical and mental health challenges, differences in socioeconomic

status, different personal experiences and personalities, fundamental social and political disagreements, and most importantly, our dislike for each other.

When we dislike and/or disagree with each other, we don't seem able to consistently show love and solidarity with one another. Unfortunately, the reasons we dislike each other are what Audre Lorde calls "the master's tools." These tools are thoughts, feelings, behaviors, and actions that strengthen white terrorism and global anti-blackness. We have been duped, tricked, lied to, bamboozled, and brainwashed to believe that the ways of white people are the right ways. We have been indoctrinated into the sick narrative that "white is right," and we still consider the American Dream to consist of working for what white folks have. We have been conditioned to hate other Black people simply for not being white people.

We too have been subjugated to the deadly white anesthesia that I talk about when I'm teaching classes on why white folks are violent and terroristic. I use the analogy of a fishbowl to describe this truth, and it goes like this: when white people are born, they are immediately dropped into the fishbowl. And they are the only ones there; every nonwhite human being lives outside the fishbowl. The fishbowl's water consists of three powerful and toxic elements: white violence, anti-blackness, and anesthesia. White people swim in this water every single day of their lives. Most white folks will dwell in the toxic water until they die; they are committed to being racist. Some white folks will occasionally peek their head out to try to escape this lethal concoction, but then they'll realize they can't breathe or survive without it. They believe themselves to be good, liberal white people, but they are actively complicit in the crimes committed against Black people. A few white folks will leap outside the fishbowl to become anti-racist "allies" and to begin to detoxify themselves so they can be fully human. Remember, the true human beings live outside the fishbowl.

Between the years of 1619 and roughly 1965 (specifically, the years of chattel slavery, Reconstruction, and Jim Crow), Black people were forced to swim inside the fishbowl with white people. During that time, Black folks were held captive within the deadly concoction of white terrorism, and as a result, they were indoctrinated into the fishbowl prescription of how to engage with others. While in this fishbowl, Black people learned how to hate, harm, and abuse each other. We learned how to be anti-black. And for generations after the Emancipation Proclamation was enacted, Black folks taught their children these same toxic tactics. Unfortunately, I too was taught many of these master's tools, and I blindly taught some of them to my son when he was younger. Fortunately for me and my family, my indoctrination was only temporarily successful.

Let me explain this indoctrination another way: white folks forced my great-great-great-grandmother into the toxic fishbowl and overtly and vicariously taught her how to hate, harm, and abuse her fellow Black people. She taught her daughter Harriet (my great-great-grandmother), Harriet taught her daughter Rachel (my great-grandmother), Rachel taught her daughter Sally (my grandmother), Sally taught her daughter Robbie (my mother), Robbie taught her daughter (me), and I taught my son. Seven generations! At a minimum. Brainwashed!

This indoctrination, this brainwashing, is at least seven generations deep in my family. Now multiply that by every Black person in America (specifically, those of us who are descendants of enslaved Africans), and you will see the magnitude of the virulent, toxic fishbowl and its malignant manifestations. And while I know every Black person is different and we are not a monolith, this thread of truth is just that: true for all of us. We have been generationally indoctrinated, and some of us do not want to lose our conditioning. Some of us don't want to unlearn these toxic tactics, and some of us resist the others who have chosen to no longer be intoxicated by the sick and callous concoction of white terroristic thought. For many of us, getting drunk off this killer Kool-Aid and remaining inebriated makes us feel better and more powerful than our fellow Black folks.

There was an embarrassing time when I would drink pitcher after pitcher of that deadly drink. Well... I didn't know what I didn't know. No one taught me how to unlearn this indoctrination, or even that I was indoctrinated. I sought out the resources to unlearn it, and I am still on a journey of unlearning, which is a vital part of my self-love journey today. And I am sure no one taught the women before me how to unlearn this conditioning. Today I am helping my son unlearn what I now regret I taught him, and I am encouraging him to not condition his children with white toxic thoughts.

We will not win, and we will not achieve liberation, by wielding the master's tools against one another (weaponizing internalized anti-blackness and toxic whiteness), using white toxic thoughts, or forcing this indoctrination down our children's and grandchildren's throats. I love this quote by James Baldwin: *"It took many years of vomiting up all the filth I'd been taught about myself, and half-believed, before I was able to walk on the earth as though I had a right to be here."* This potent truth speaks exactly to the point I have been making. What Baldwin vomited up was poison. Intentional and deliberate poison, fed to us ever since we were brought to this continent. We too must detoxify ourselves and stop drinking this pernicious poison, and we must stop letting our children get drunk on our vapors. Love. Love of self, love for our fellow Black people, and love for the Black community are what will get us free. Global Kinship Love. It is the first step in the unification of the collective Black body. The revolution will be love! It must be anchored in love.

Black love. Kinship Love does not mean we will all agree on everything, nor does it mean we will like each other in the process. Yet we can and must be empathetic to the collective Black struggle for justice, freedom, and liberation. Kinship Love means solidarity despite our differences. This is our communal fiber. The strongest and most critical one. The Movement for Black Lives is counting on us to figure this out and master it for swift, effective, and long-term community change. Even when I seem to not get along with certain Black folks, what I can do is release them with love and still fight for them and alongside them in the struggle. Remember that a critical component of releasing with love is to do and wish those people no harm, and to still love them from a distance. That is Kinship Love. So, the revolution *can* be love... you must not plot against those you've released.

The revolution *is* love. Second to self-love, Kinship Love is the most vital type of love we must create, cultivate, sustain, and pass on. One way we do this is through community building. We can be

in community even when we dislike each other. We must take no shit and do no harm while refusing to pick up the master's tools (also known as Weapons of Whiteness™). We can focus on healing and liberation instead of fighting with each other. We must hold each other accountable with compassion and grace. We can set boundaries and act with a spirit of accountability and love to amplify racial justice and Black love. We must agree to disagree without demonizing one another, so we can work toward collective healing and justice, freedom, and liberation.

This is the way forward. Of course, the list of other things to do may be long, but I believe Black love and Kinship Love are the foundations for everything else. From these foundations, we can then create, cultivate, and sustain our economics, political power, education, and healthcare systems. We can build and rebuild our communities. We can truly mean *"We all we got"* by walking the talk. In my book *Weapons of Whiteness™*, I share my personal strategy, which I call the *Catriceology® Way*. It is my six-step method for being a conscious conduit for Black unification and Black liberation. The following is a list of my action steps; see the Resources section of this book for detailed information about each step:

1. Give Black people compassion and grace.

2. Take no shit and do no harm.

3. Release people with love.

4. Know who is with you versus who is for you.

5. Let people eat even if it's not at your table.

6. Choose accountability and love.

We really are all we've got. Although we can dislike each other while still being in community with each other, I am hoping what I have shared in this book will help you feel more genuine and consistent affection for your fellow Black people. Regardless, being in community is key to all of us getting free and liberated once and for all from toxic whiteness. This is the Catriceology Way, and maybe this strategy and its commitments will help you while you create your own way.

We literally have too many other battles to fight; we shouldn't waste our time or energies fighting each other. And we certainly won't win the war this way. Love is the only way we win. The revolution will be love. We can fight for *freedom*, but if we don't love each other once we're free, what's the point? The revolution will be love. We can fight for *justice*, but if we don't love each other after the police arrest us, we remain in their jails. We can fight for *liberation*, but if we return to our own homes after the victory and abuse each other, are we truly liberated? The Movement for Black Lives will die without love. And if there is no love in it, it will not succeed.

Loving the community and movement is not enough. If you don't love *yourself* when you show up in the community and the movement, you will contaminate them. If you love *only* yourself when you show up in the community and the movement, you will contaminate them. The Movement for Black Lives is only as powerful as the people who love themselves and the others in the movement. Black love has to become the priority. Single folks must love themselves more. Couples must work on loving each other more. Parents must love their children more, and children must love their parents more. And we must show more love to our elders, because their time with us is limited. Love is the revolution!

- Black love is mutual respect, admiration, authenticity, integrity, emotional intimacy, trust, and honesty.

- Black love is compassion, affinity, connectedness, solidarity, acceptance, empathy, and altruism.

- Black love is attraction, passion, devotion, intimacy, affection, desire, and vulnerability.

- Black love is loyalty, reciprocity, gratitude, and reverence.

- Black love is Rafiki Love, Kinship Love, Romantic Love, and Soul Love.

The revolution will be love. We will triumph over our trials and tribulations through love. We will conquer our challenges with love. We will heal through love. We will build with love. We will win the war through love. Black people united, loving on each other all over the world—*that* is the revolution.

And while love can be complicated and textured, don't be afraid of it. Cynicism and fear create anguish. Fear is the opposite of love. Fear constricts while love expands. Fear sabotages while love multiplies. Fear keeps you captive while love sets you free. True liberation is rooted in love and cannot happen without it.

- Don't be afraid to love.

- Love redeems. Love inspires. Love empowers.

- Love is not perfect, nor is it pain-free.

- When imperfect people engage in love, there are bound to be misunderstandings, heartbreak, and grief.

- Love is both pleasure and pain. It takes courage and vulnerability to love yourself and others.

- Remember that love, Black love, is a Beautiful Struggle.
- Remember that love is how you choose to define it, live it, give it, and receive it.
- Remember that love looks good on you, and you deserve it.
- Embrace love and bask in its glory. Let it feed and nourish you.
- Allow love to heal and strengthen you.
- Let love be your constant fuel, fire, fortitude, and fortress.
- Let love enrich every part of your life.
- Let love hold you and nurture you.
- Love has sustained us, and it will be love that returns us to ourselves.
- Love prevails. The revolution is love; it will always be love.
- Without love, there will be no justice, because justice is love.

And I hope you always choose blackness.

I hope you choose it even when it doesn't choose you. Because we all we got!

Keep choosing Black love. Embrace it. Embody it. Nurture it.

And when you're lost in fear, doubt, and struggle, choose love, and let it return you to yourself. Let love bring you home.

Above all else… love.

It's the one thing whiteness can't take from us.

Let love in. Be love…

I love you.

Inhale.

Exhale.

Asé!

## LOVE JUICE

*Love is allowing love to be your fuel, fire, fortitude, and fortress for the revolution.*

—*Catriceology*

## LOVE NOTES

What conditioning and indoctrination do you need to unlearn so you can be free of toxic whiteness?

_____

_____

_____

_____

How do you plan to strengthen your Kinship Love to enrich your affinity with your Black siblings of the African diaspora?

_____

_____

_____

_____

_____

The revolution is love. How will you lead your own personal love revolution?

_____

_____

_____

_____

# The Catriceology Way

*"We don't have to like each other to be in community,
but we can love each other and do no harm."*

**Catrice M. Jackson**

This section first appeared in my book *Weapons of Whiteness™: Exposing the Master's Tools Behind the Mask of Anti-Blackness*.

Both parts of this section's quote are true, and they can exist simultaneously. There is no perfect or right strategy for Black unification and Black liberation, and that's due to our never-ending wounding from whiteness. The trauma we experience from whiteness and the trauma we create for each other keep us trapped in a perpetual cycle of violence. We exist in a space of constant fight, flight, and freeze, leaving little or no room for compassion, grace, healing, or joy. And just as I tell white folks, it's going to take a lifetime to rid ourselves of toxic whiteness and anti-blackness. This must be our most pressing call to action, and we must prioritize it and make it the center of our attention and intention, because fighting, fleeing, and freezing will not promote our healing, and those actions sure won't liberate us.

We love to holler, *"We all we got,"* but do we really believe it? Truthfully, we *are* all we got, and we got to start living it. I will be the first to say I have yet to master this truth, so I work on being consistent with my thoughts by showing up in what I call the *"Catriceology® Way."*

The Catriceology Way is my personal strategy to be a conscious conduit for Black unification and Black liberation. In this section, I share the top six personal commitments I have made to Black people and how I walk out those commitments.

## 1. Give Black people compassion and grace

White terrorism and anti-blackness are baked into America's foundation, and so is our history of forgiving white folks. Hell, Black people have been forced to forgive them or suffer dire consequences for four hundred years. Forgiving white folks for their violence is a form of self-abuse we have been conditioned to commit. Isn't it bad enough we have to endure their violence? Being forced or trained to also have to forgive them for it is straight-up sinister. It's abusive, and after centuries of conditioning, it's now second nature for us. I have chosen to shift my capacity for compassion and grace to Black people. I especially reserve those attributes for them. White folks don't automatically receive compassion and grace from me; they have to earn them. And white people who don't value and appreciate my compassion and grace lose them.

My compassion and grace for Black folks look like me being more patient with them, forgiving them for their ignorance, ignoring comments I'm willing to let slide, and not holding grudges when they harm me. I don't always do this, and when I do, I don't always do it perfectly. That's because like you, I'm on my own personal journeys of ridding myself from toxic whiteness and anti-blackness and working to be a better human being.

*How will you show Black people more compassion and grace?*

_____

_____

_____

_____

## 2. Take no shit and do no harm

Just because I offer Black people more compassion and grace than I do white people, it does not mean I'm willing to be a pushover or a doormat. Just like you, I deserve to set boundaries and have them respected. When people do not want to respect my boundaries, then it is not worth my time to have those people in my life. I receive the most attacks from white women; the group I receive the second-highest amount of harm from is Black women. And if I am honest, they are the group of people I've knowingly and unknowingly caused the most harm to. This is because Black women have been taught to work against each other. We have been taught to compete with one another, and we have been conditioned to hate on each other.

We must undo this learning. We must teach ourselves, for the first time, to love each other despite our differences and conflicts. We have to stop competing and learn to collaborate with each other, and when we cannot collaborate, then we must do no harm. I believe in taking no shit and doing no harm. We can disagree and still love one another, and that's what I try to do every day. I give Black people a lot of compassion and grace, and even when they come for me, I don't seek revenge in any way. Ever.

*What boundaries do you need to set, and what commitments do you need to make with yourself, so you can take no shit and do no harm?*

_____

_____

_____

_____

### 3. Release people with love

I must say I have mastered releasing people with love. When I say "release," I mean let people go emotionally, physically, and socially. Especially on social media. As soon as I realize another Black person doesn't mean me well, isn't good for my mental health, and/or they've made it very clear they have no interest in engaging with me or valuing our connection, I release them. When people don't appreciate my presence, I allow them to enjoy my absence. Most times I just go away quietly and stop engaging with them. Sometimes I give compassion and grace for too long, and then it takes me longer to release a person. But once I release them, they are released. On a few occasions, I have agreed to let them back in, but in most cases, another release happens shortly thereafter.

It is okay to release people. We are not all going to agree with, get along with, and/or like each other, and that is perfectly fine if we can release each other with love. By "with love," I mean just let them go and wish them well. No dragging. No smear campaigns. No gossiping. No vendettas or revenge. Nothing. Let them go and keep it moving. "With love" means you wish them no harm, and you hope they prosper and thrive. "With love" also means you love yourself enough to release

whatever is heavy and weighing down your spirit. Sometimes it is necessary to let folks know you are releasing them, and other times you should just walk away without making a big scene. Each person you release requires a unique approach. But do not hold grudges. Don't stay connected if people are toxic, refuse to respect your boundaries, treat you like you don't matter, and/or fail to treat you with dignity and respect. Release them with love.

*What does releasing people with love look like for you?*

_____

_____

_____

_____

## 4. Know who is with you versus who is for you

I am still perfecting this commitment. It is important to be able to quickly discern who is *with* you versus who is *for* you. People who are *with* you are just that: they are with you for the benefits their association with you brings. They are folks who want to be close to you for some type of advantage or perk. They want to gain access to your thoughts, ideas, plans, people, resources, and perceived clout. People who are with you want to be in your presence for personal gain, not mutual benefit. They often have hidden motives. In the beginning, they often appear very interested in you, are quite supportive, will shower you with compliments, and give you lots of pats on the back. They often present as a "real" friend, but soon they either go silent and/or the sweet behaviors turn salty. They stop engaging. They throw shade. Or they

straight-up start dragging your name. This is often the result of either their motives not being met and/or your realization they are not really *for* you.

Because when people are *for* you, their only motive is they genuinely care for and like you. They have no hidden agendas. They are not looking to gain anything but your friendship. People who are for you believe in and practice reciprocity in relationships. They know how to give and take. They easily give you the same (or similar) energy and support you give them. The only things they truly want for you is for you to thrive and be successful, and they are often willing to help you achieve your goals. Folks who are for you love you, whether you have something to give them or not, or whether they have something to gain or not, by being your friend. People who are for you are the ones to keep around. They are real friends. The sooner you can discern this about people, the less trauma and stress you'll experience.

*What are the signs that tell you someone is for you?*

_____

_____

_____

_____

### 5. Let people eat even if it's not at your table

Everyone deserves to eat. Including people you don't like or get along with. No matter how much I may not like or get along with another Black person, I am committed to doing no harm, especially by trying to block their ability to survive and thrive. This means I don't

slander their name, and I don't do anything else that would prevent them from healing or getting what they need to thrive in life. Your table is not the only table from which folks can eat. And if for some reason you choose to not feed someone or let them sit at your table (be in community with you), don't try to stop them from creating their own table or eating at someone else's. I have personally experienced a Black woman who tried to block the bounty by discrediting my name. What I know is she cannot block blessings that are mine. I believe whatever is meant for me is truly meant for me, even if people may try to prevent me from getting it.

When you release people with love from your table, you do not block their bounty or try to make them starve. Conversely, releasing people with love allows for good karma to come your way. It is the law of reciprocity. When you do other people dirty, that dirt will come back to you in one way or another. I know it's sometimes hard to release folks with love—with the hope they can create or find another table—but the more you do it, the better you get at it. And the better you become as a person. Try it. Often.

*If there is someone you don't want eating at your table, how can you make sure they are still able to eat?*

---

---

---

---

## 6. Choose accountability and love

When conflicts arise between me and other Black people, my first thought is to act with accountability and love. In my opinion, accountability is not a bad thing, and when it is done with intention and care, it can save many relationships and friendships that are on the brink of breaking. When conflicts arise, use accountability and love to address the person's *behavior*, not the person. Accountability is about holding people responsible by requesting that they not only take ownership of their behavior, but also create a plan to reconcile their offense.

Accountability may or may not include the goal of remaining connected; however, atonement is definitely a desired outcome. When you hold someone accountable with love, there is no need for an audience or public display of dragging. You don't need to bring anyone else into the situation either, unless they are directly involved. Just keep the focus on you and the person who caused harm. When you hold someone accountable with love, there is no need for name calling, defamation, or destruction. Love does not use Weapons of Whiteness™. Love seeks repentance. Love is hopeful. Love seeks resolve. Love is a win/win.

When others hurt us, it's hard to choose love. I don't always choose it, but I'm getting better at doing so more consistently. When we pick up the Weapons of Whiteness and use them on one another, those are not acts of love, those are the master's tools. And we will never dismantle the master's house by using his violence against each other. Using accountability and love with each other opens the pathway for all of us to heal. This is another way we rid ourselves of toxic whiteness. This is another way we bring about freedom and liberation.

*What are some situations you're currently dealing with for which you need to choose accountability and love?*

_____

_____

_____

_____

We really are all we've got. Although we can dislike each other while still being in community with each other, I am hoping what I have shared in this book will help you feel more genuine and consistent affection for your fellow Black people. Regardless, being in community is key to all of us getting free and liberated once and for all from toxic whiteness. This is the Catriceology Way, and maybe this strategy and its commitments will help you while you create your own way. One last thing: I hope you always choose blackness. I hope you choose it even when it doesn't choose you. Because we all we got!

> I love you!
> In solidarity.

> *"It is our duty to fight for our freedom.*
> *It is our duty to win.*
> *We must love each other and support each other.*
> *We have nothing to lose but our chains."*
> —Assata Shakur, *Assata: An Autobiography*

# We All We Got – Unf*ckablewith

This poem first appeared in my book *Unf*ckablewith: Rising From the Ashes Into Your Black Woman Badassery*. Although it is addressed to Black women, its message is for all Black people.

*I can't breathe.*
*I can't breathe.*
*I can't breathe!*
*Too loud.*
*Too dark.*
*Too light.*
*Too bossy.*
*I can't breathe.*
*Too independent.*
*Too ratchet.*
*Too bougie.*
*Too ghetto.*
*I can't breathe.*
*No, you can't touch my hair.*
*No, I ain't your mammy.*
*No, I won't be your footstool.*
*Damn, I can't breathe.*
*I can't breathe.*
*Too strong.*

*Too bold.*

*I'm tired.*

*I can't breathe.*

*Stop touching me.*

*Leave me alone.*

*No, I don't want to explain.*

*What the hell you looking at?*

*I can't breathe.*

*Can I just live?*

*White toxicity consuming all the space.*

*Get out of my way.*

*Damn, can I get a seat at the table?*

*Ain't I a woman?*

*Get off my neck!*

*I can't f*cking breathe!*

*I'm dying...*

*Yes, it's my real hair!*

*Get your hands off my mouth.*

*Stop silencing me.*

*I'm tired.*

*I can't breathe.*

*Yes, I'm angry.*

*Sick of folks pressuring me.*

*Do you hear me screaming?*

*No, I won't move out the way.*

*I don't owe you a smile.*

*I don't owe you shit!*

*Did you hear me say I can't breathe!*
*I'm tired of being woke.*
*Why are you staring at me?*
*I'm falling, y'all!*
*Do you hear me?*
*Do you see me?*
*I said I can't breathe!*
*I don't owe you nothing.*
*I'm not your negro!*
*I'm tired of shucking and jiving!*
*Whew...*
*I can't catch my breath.*
*I'm losing it.*
*So tired.*
*Stop touching my children.*
*What'd you say to me?*
*Watch my tone?*
*Damn.*
*Can I catch my breath?*
*I can't breathe. I can't freaking breathe!*
*I'm dying.*
*Can you see my pain?*
*No, I won't teach you.*
*I'm not a resource.*
*Can I just have some joy?*
*No, I won't wait my turn!*
*No, I won't shrink.*

*I'm drowning, y'all.*

*I'm tired.*

*You too, Sis?*

*You causing me pain, too?*

*Not you too, Black Woman.*

*It hurts!*

*Damn.*

*Ain't no safe place for Black women.*

*It's too much.*

*I can't take it.*

*Sick of shifting and shuffling.*

*My feet hurt.*

*I'm exhausted.*

*I can't breathe!*

*Damn, another Black person killed?*

*Stop killing us!*

*Does anybody care?*

*Who is going to protect us?*

*Stop bumping into me.*

*I do not have to concede.*

*No, I don't work here!*

*Why are you following me?*

*Do you see my tears?*

*I'm weak.*

*I'm overwhelmed!*

*Somebody help me!*

*Please!*

*Whew...*

*Whew...*

*I'm suffocating.*

*Gasp...*

*Silence...*

*Wait, Sis!*

*Keep breathing.*

*Don't you quit.*

*Don't you give up.*

*I got you.*

*Get up, Sis.*

*You are not alone.*

*I know your pain.*

*Your rage is justified.*

*Here, have some of my breath.*

*My strength.*

*Lean on me.*

*I got you.*

*Get up.*

*You can make it through this.*

*Let me carry you for a while.*

*I see you. I hear you.*

*Don't let them kill you!*

*Puff...*

*Puff...*

*Puff...*

*Sis.*

*Inhale.*

*Breathe.*

*C'mon, Sister.*

*You are a Queen.*

*Do you know who you are?*

*Puff...*

*Puff...*

*Puff...*

*You are valuable.*

*You matter.*

*I love you.*

*I need you.*

*You need you.*

*We need you.*

*C'mon, Sis.*

*I love you, Sis.*

*Don't give up.*

*There is royalty in your blood.*

*You got dreams to fulfill.*

*Breathe!*

*Breathe!*

*Breathe!*

*Your destiny is waiting for you.*

*You don't have to do it alone.*

*I know you're tired.*

*It's okay to be vulnerable.*

*I got you.*

*Puff...*

*Puff...*

*Puff...*

*Gasp...*

*Whew!*

*Whew!*

*Inhale...*

*Exhale...*

*You're breathing!*

*Inhale.*

*Open your eyes, Sis!*

*You can breathe.*

*Take a deep breath.*

*Hold on to me.*

*I got you.*

*Stand up.*

*Stand on the shoulders of your ancestors!*

*They are with you.*

*I am with you.*

*Breathe.*

*Breathe, Sis!*

*Rise up.*

*Rise up!*

*Yes!*

*That's right. You can do this!*

*Rise up, Sis!*

*From those ashes...*

*Don't let the fire consume you!*
*Yes, you're standing up!*
*Hold your head up.*
*Breathe!*
*Rise up!*
*Rise.*
*Up.*

*I don't know what kind of ashes you may be standing in right now.*
*I don't know the pain you might be experiencing.*
*I don't know your struggles and fears.*
*I don't know what you're going through.*
*But I do know this: you don't have to go through it alone.*
*I know you're valuable and you matter.*
*I know what the fire feels like.*
*I've been through storms, too.*
*I know your rage is justified.*
*I know the fire can consume you if you let it.*
*I know you can rise from your ashes.*
*I know you can become the fire.*
*I will go through the storm with you.*
*I will rage with you. I will become the fire with you.*
*I'm here with and for you.*
*I got you.*

*It's time to rise up, Sis!*

*Rise up and go on this journey into the dimensions of Unf\*ckablewith with me.*

*It's time.*

*It's time to rise up into your Black Woman Badassery!*

*Let's go.*

# Black People

*I love Black people!*

> *Cornrows, twists, locs, and taper fades.*
>
> *Afro puffs and coils.*
>
> *Doo rags, Black Power fist picks, and hood swag.*

*I love Black people!*

> *Gospel music on Sunday mornings.*
>
> *Grits, collard greens, and sweet potato pie.*
>
> *Hip hop.*
>
> *The Harlem Renaissance.*
>
> *Rock and roll, doo-wop, R&B, and soul.*

*I love Black people!*

> *Snapbacks, dashikis, and bean pies.*
>
> *Lady Sings the Blues, the electric slide, and Langston Hughes.*
>
> *By any means necessary, Do the Right Thing, melanin poppin' Black Girl Magic, and that new jack swing!*
>
> *"Back That Thang Up," "Knuck If You Buck," black-eyed peas, and rolling trees.*
>
> *Jumping the broom, Big Mama and nem, Cousin Ray Ray, and Training Day.*

*I love Black people!*

> *Multifaceted and multitalented innovative geniuses.*
>
> *Bringing flavor to everything.*
>
> *Kings and queens.*

*Birthed from the cradle of humanity, rooted in the motherland, and first on all lands.*

*No one does it like we do it, and it don't matter what "it" is.*

*We salt of the earth.*

*Fragments of the universe.*

*Cosmic.*

*Creative.*

*Glorious.*

*Naturally dope!*

*Black love is beautiful.*

*Black love is essential.*

*I love Black people!*

*We are beauty and love in motion.*

*We are a glorious dance with the universe. We **are** the universe.*

*We are a melanated mosaic of the majestic God/Goddess.*

*Head wraps, Bid Whist, and Spades. Box braids and silk presses.*

*Double Dutch and jump rope in front of the stoop.*

*We are the original cool.*

*We are the dream. We are our ancestors' wildest dreams.*

*We are a Black fist moment.*

*We are the Movement for Black Lives.*

*Because Black Lives Matter.*

*Rosewood.*

*Black Wall Street and the "Letter from Birmingham Jail."*

*Black love is resistance.*

*Black love is persistence.*

*Black love will prevail even in the struggle.*

*I love Black people!*

"No justice, no peace."

We will continue to march in the streets.

And we will continue to demand that Black love be uninhibited and celebrated.

Black love is powerful.

Black love inspires.

Black love heals.

I love Black people!

And we get to choose it in every moment.

We get to choose to love ourselves.

We get to choose to love each other.

We get to choose to love our families and our communities.

Black love is beautiful; it is you and me.

Black love; that's who we be.

# 50 Ways To Be More Courageous

Here are fifty tips for you to live more courageously, from my book *The Art of Fear-Free Living: Awaken the Geni(us) Within.*

1. Make a list of the things you need to forgive yourself for, and then, one by one, release the shame, guilt, and regret.

2. Identify the people in your life you need to forgive. Choose to do the work within your heart to forgive them.

3. Start a courage journal, write down all the things you want to do, and find creative ways to make them happen.

4. Choose the risks you can take now to be more courageous.

5. Remember not only the moments when you were wise and strong, but also how you were able to create success in those moments.

6. Make a list of the values and standards you want to live by, and start living by them.

7. Think about everything in your life you don't like or want to do, and create your "not to do" list. Be brave and just stop doing those things.

8. Use your fears to drive you toward your passion and purpose.

9. When you become aware of fear, remember that the awareness of fear is a signal that something is missing from your life.

10. See the same significance in feeding your soul as you do in feeding your body. Determine how you will feed your soul every day.

11. Check your emotional energy tank, and determine who is filling it or causing you to run on fumes. Determine what you can do to remove the energy stealers in your life, and do it.

12. Decide what you can do every day to move from surviving to thriving in your life.

13. Every time you feel fearful, ask yourself, "What is the worst that could happen if I do not face this fear, and what is the worst that could happen if I *do* face this fear?" You'll see you have more to lose by NOT facing your fears.

14. Remember, you have only two choices in life: be afraid and live afraid, or be fearless and live courageously.

15. Instead of focusing your energy on your fears, focus your energy on how you can get the resources you need to conquer them.

16. Color your life's canvas with vibrant, energetic, and happy people who can keep you inspired while you master the art of fear-free living.

17. Remember, every day you have the choice to take down the old, dull, gray canvas and put up a blank one to create your fearless life.

18. Know your personal power is like a big eraser. You have the power to erase the negative thoughts about yourself, the past hurts that are keeping you stuck, and everything in your life that is causing you distress and misery.

19. As you begin to create a fearless life, remember you already have the tools you need within you—you just have to seek them out and use them.

20. Be mindful to stay off autopilot. Instead, live each moment of your life fully awake.

21. Make it a personal priority to ask yourself every day, "What do I need to face, and how can I face it not only with the resources I have, but also with ease and grace?

22. Be intentional in every moment. Engage only in activities and conversations that move you one step closer to your goals.

23. Remember, facing your fears is simply about taking risks, and you must be willing to take some risks to get what you desire.

24. Create a vision board, and fill it up with words, pictures, and quotes that depict how you want to live your fearless life.

25. Create your fearless life dream team: a small group of dedicated, positive, and trustworthy people who believe in you and your ? dreams, and who will help you bring your dreams to life.

26. Be mindful to not make excuses for not doing something that can empower your life. Excuses are doorways to failure.

27. When faced with a fear, instead of allowing yourself to worry and become paralyzed, seek out the resources to help you conquer the fear.

28. Be curious. When fear shows up, ask yourself, "I wonder what would happen if I faced this fear?" Be still and listen for the answer that comes from your heart.

29. Accept that you will have obstacles in your life, and begin to see them as opportunities to strengthen yourself.

30. Instead of dreading facing your fears, wake up each day with gratitude and ask yourself, "How can I be brave today?" And then take action.

31. *Unsubscribe!* That's right: opt out of everything that does not fill your cup, fulfill you, serve your highest good, and/or take you one step closer to your highest self.

32. Surrender once a day. In the morning, surrender to the Universe, and let God order your steps. In the evening, surrender again, and release all the toxicity you've taken in during the day.

33. Choose to be struggle-free! Struggle brings pain and frustration, which are not worth paying for with your life.

34. Be accepting. Sometimes you've simply got to say, "It is what it is." Let it go and keep it moving.

35. Quit looking for the answers. Instead, let them just come to you, and enjoy life while you wait for the divine downloads to occur.

36. Trust yourself more. Trust what you need will come. Trust you know yourself better than anyone else. Stop fighting yourself; instead, just trust yourself.

37. Take action! Worrying, contemplating, agonizing, and analyzing are signs of struggle. Ask your heart and your soul whether you should act, and if you feel peace, then get out of your head and take action.

38. Learn how to filter out the background noise. The background noise is other people's opinions, demands, and requests. It's your life; do what you want to do, and make your own decisions.

39. Release the need to be perfect or right. There's no such thing as perfect, and you will never be right all the time. Instead, strive to be the best you can be without measuring yourself against anyone. Remember, being wrong means you're human.

40. When you stop judging others, you will learn to accept them for who they are. And this in turn allows you to start accepting *yourself* for who you are.

41. Your past is a part of who you are, but it does not determine who you will become. Let go and be free, or keep holding on and be miserable.

42. Take out a new canvas every day and start over. Yesterday is gone and is a memory. Tomorrow may never come and is a dream. Today is all you have and is a blessing.

43. Every day you have a choice to stay captive or to be brave. Take out your courage key and unlock your life. Stop wallowing in "what if" and begin basking in your bravery.

44. Look for at least one opportunity each day to grow and evolve. Read a new book, write in your journal—it doesn't matter what you do, as long as it takes you one step closer to fearless living.

45. Get over yourself! Someone out there has it worse than you do. While you are indeed important, the world does not revolve around you.

46. Fearless living is about survival of the fittest. Either you change, grow, and evolve, or life will pass you by. Get up and get into your life.

47. You can't change everything in your life with one choice, but the choice to live fearlessly can make a dramatic change.

48. Choose to live deliciously! Write down your recipe for a delicious life on a real recipe card. Get creative and add in a little spice, passion, excitement, satisfaction, and zest, and you are sure to whip up a life that makes your mouth water.

49. Clock in and go to work! Living YOUR LIFE fearlessly is an inside job. It's the most important job you will ever have in your life. Go in early, work hard, take on extra projects, be on the leadership team, put in one hundred percent effort, stay late, clock out, and start all over again. When you work this job like it's the only one you'll ever have, the recognition, raises, and promotions are guaranteed.

50. Decide what you want, how you want to be, and how you want to live your life, and then get it, be it, and live it. The only thing keeping you from living a rewarding and fulfilling life is you. Tell your ego to get out of the way, and allow the best version of yourself to reign in your life. It's your life—own it, create it, live it, and love it—fearlessly!

# Unleash Your Magic:
# What Is Magic?

These definitions of YOUR magic appeared in my books *Unleash Your Significance: Activate the Audacity to Be All You Are Destined to Be* and *The Becky Code: Don't Waste Your Magic*.

Do you know how powerful and special YOUR magic is? *You are rare and can never be duplicated, ever!* That is pure magic all by itself. Can you imagine what your life will be like when you embrace this powerful truth? You are rare, pure magic! So, what is magic?

- Magic is turning your words into experiences.

- Magic is moving a dream from distant thought to an intimate reality.

- Magic is making the invisible tangible and touchable.

- Magic is predicting how your life turns out.

- Magic is transforming your physical body and restoring your vitality.

- Magic is purging your soul from everything that paralyzes your purpose.

- Magic is doing work you love and loving the work you do.

- Magic is leaping out of your comfort zone into the unknown, and thriving.

- Magic is turning limiting beliefs into limitless possibilities.

- Magic is creating harmony within and living your own unique melody.

- Magic is creating and experiencing moments that take your breath away.

- Magic is trusting that your soul knows the way and following it.

- Magic is saying "so what" and living your life unapologetically.

- Magic is slowing down and savoring the silence and synchronicity of life.

- Magic is hearing the whispers of the divine one and saying "yes!"

- Magic is unleashing your gifts and serving the world with them.

- Magic is *not giving a damn* what other people think of you.

- Magic is making a meaningful contribution to humanity.

- Magic is fiercely loving you better than anyone else ever could.

- Magic is following your bliss and wallowing in all the goodness and splendor you can imagine.

- Magic is having peace of mind, love in your heart, and a generous spirit.

- Magic is deeply forgiving yourself and choosing to love and be loved again.

- Magic is being comfortable in your own skin and appreciating every magnificent part of yourself.

- Magic is thinking positive thoughts and showing up in the world with optimism.

- Magic is curiosity, creativity, and answering your life's calling.

*Magic is unlimited!* There are so many ways to create magic in your life in your own unique way. Please stop trying to duplicate someone else's life. You'll never live their dreams. You'll never walk their path. You'll never carry out their purpose, and you'll never arrive at their destination. Embrace the awesomeness of your originality, manifest your own dreams, confidently walk your own path, and live out your special destiny that's designed just for you!

# Words To Inspire Your Core Values

This powerful activity has appeared in several of my previous books. One of the ways I stay grounded in my truth and remain *Unf*ckablewith* is by establishing and living by five core values. I use these values as the foundation for how I choose to show up in the world, and as guiding principles for how I want to live my life. My core values are *Authenticity, Freedom, Truth, Peace,* and *Inspiration.* I've been using these five words to navigate my best life since 2010. I encourage you to choose five foundational words that best represent the core of who you are and how you want to navigate your life. The words you choose should serve as the pillars of your unwavering way of being, and they should represent the truth of who you are. Here are a few words to inspire the creation of your core values.

| | | |
|---|---|---|
| Creativity | Inspiration | Fantasy |
| Innovation | Focus | Meaning |
| Fascination | Glory | Curiosity |
| Serendipity | Exploration | Love |
| Vibrancy | Magnetism | Peace |
| Gratitude | Joy | Abundance |
| Prosperity | Security | Safety |
| Laughter | Excitement | Adventure |
| Compassion | Passion | Faith |
| Serenity | Purpose | Clarity |

| | | |
|---|---|---|
| Optimism | Determination | Grace |
| Courage | Bravery | Appreciation |
| Beauty | Contribution | Satisfaction |
| Service | Generosity | Empathy |
| Wisdom | Belief | Happiness |
| Fun | Connection | Trust |
| Flow | Synchronicity | Harmony |
| Intention | Luxury | Truth |
| Magic | Vitality | Play |
| Aliveness | Relaxation | Imagination |
| Confidence | Delight | Leisure |
| Freedom | Calmness | Authenticity |
| Audacity | Resiliency | Ancestry |
| Impact | Discipline | Sovereignty |
| Justice | Tenacity | Transformation |

# Writing Prompts To Rise From the Ashes

These writing prompts appeared in my books *Unleash Your Significance: Activate the Audacity to Be All You Are Destined to Be* and *Weapons of Whiteness™: Exposing the Master's Tools Behind the Mask of Anti-Blackness.*

Use these writing prompts to help you release and process your feelings around fighting both systemic racism and anti-blackness. My hope is that these prompts will allow you to focus more on your healing and joy. I believe it's not only possible, but also necessary and urgent, that each of us rise from the ashes!

How are you allowing life to just happen instead of actively creating it?

_____

_____

_____

_____

_____

_____

_____

In what ways are you choosing to self-abuse and play the role of victim?

_____

_____

_____

_____

_____

_____

Who have been some of your teachers and what have you learned from them?

_____

_____

_____

_____

_____

What life lessons do you keep repeating that you no longer want to repeat?

_____

_____

_____

_____

_____

How do you truly feel about yourself?

_____

_____

_____

_____

_____

_____

What do you believe to be true about yourself?

_____

_____

_____

_____

_____

_____

Who do you need to forgive?

_____

_____

_____

_____

_____

_____

In what areas of your life do you need to take full responsibility and stop blaming others?

_____

_____

_____

_____

_____

_____

What kind of conditioning have you experienced that you want to unlearn?

_____

_____

_____

_____

_____

_____

What do you think your spiritual gifts are?

_____

_____

_____

_____

_____

What would you like to see in the panoramic view of your life?

_____

_____

_____

_____

_____

_____

What will you focus on from this point on?

_____

_____

_____

_____

_____

_____

In what ways are you settling, struggling, and living in mediocrity?

_____

_____

_____

_____

_____

_____

Who do you want to be until you take your last breath?

_____

_____

_____

_____

_____

_____

In what ways have you heard God's voice but dismissed it or didn't believe it?

_____

_____

_____

_____

_____

How would you like God to speak to you so you can take action?

_____

_____

_____

_____

_____

What did you learn from your family and upbringing that you want to unlearn so you can break the cycle?

_____

_____

_____

_____

_____

In what ways are you still living in the past?

_____

_____

_____

_____

_____

_____

How do you define success?

_____

_____

_____

_____

_____

_____

How do you define significance?

_____

_____

_____

_____

_____

_____

Are you average or extraordinary? Why?

_____

_____

_____

_____

_____

In what ways are you seeking approval from others or waiting for their permission?

_____

_____

_____

_____

_____

_____

_____

Who are you blaming and what are you blaming them for?

_____

_____

_____

_____

_____

_____

What is your personal purpose?

_____

_____

_____

_____

_____

_____

What is your global purpose?

_____

_____

_____

_____

_____

_____

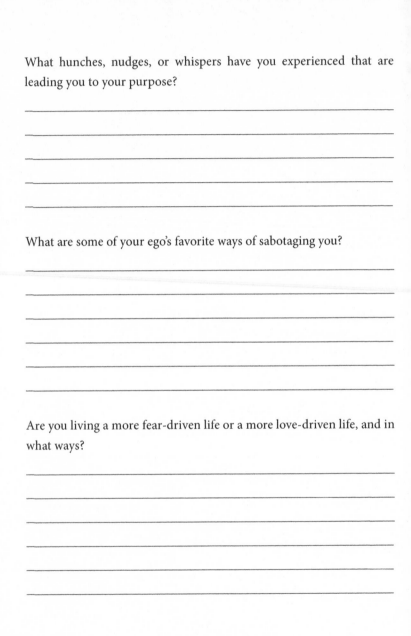

What hunches, nudges, or whispers have you experienced that are leading you to your purpose?

_____

_____

_____

_____

_____

What are some of your ego's favorite ways of sabotaging you?

_____

_____

_____

_____

_____

Are you living a more fear-driven life or a more love-driven life, and in what ways?

_____

_____

_____

_____

_____

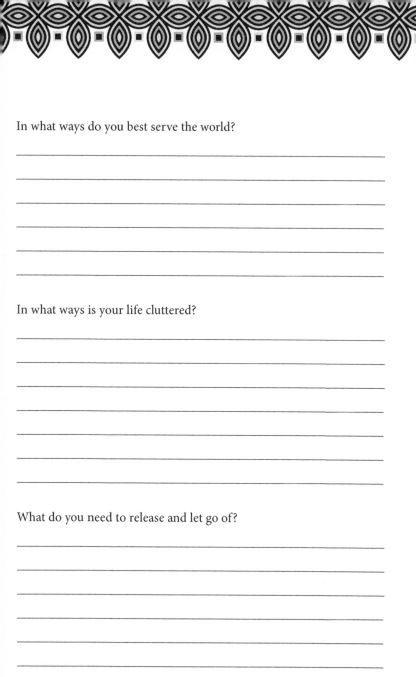

In what ways do you best serve the world?

_____

_____

_____

_____

_____

_____

In what ways is your life cluttered?

_____

_____

_____

_____

_____

_____

What do you need to release and let go of?

_____

_____

_____

_____

_____

_____

In what ways are you creating your own suffering?

_____

_____

_____

_____

_____

_____

What do you need to tell the truth about?

_____

_____

_____

_____

_____

_____

What truth do you need to know so you can move forward?

_____

_____

_____

_____

_____

_____

_____

How has being afraid affected your life?

_____

_____

_____

_____

_____

_____

What fears do you need or want to face?

_____

_____

_____

_____

_____

_____

How are you holding yourself back?

_____

_____

_____

_____

_____

_____

_____

What bricks are on top of your lid?

_____

_____

_____

_____

_____

_____

How can you step up and be the leader of your own life?

_____

_____

_____

_____

_____

_____

What is the vision for your life?

_____

_____

_____

_____

_____

_____

_____

What have you been thinking about doing that you are now willing to take action on?

_____

_____

_____

_____

_____

_____

What thinking errors (distorted thoughts) are keeping you stuck and unfulfilled in your life?

_____

_____

_____

_____

_____

How have you been comparing your life to the lives of others?

_____

_____

_____

_____

_____

_____

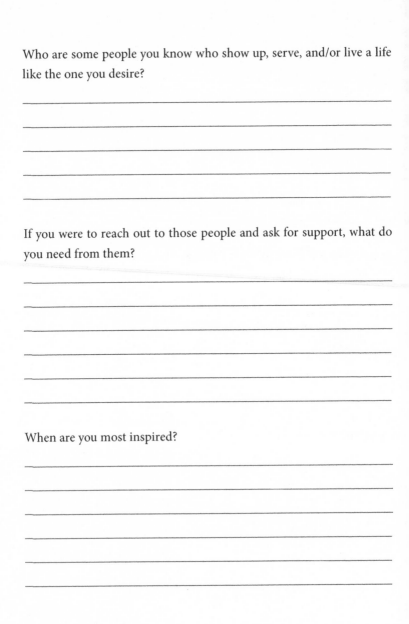

Who are some people you know who show up, serve, and/or live a life like the one you desire?

_____

_____

_____

_____

_____

If you were to reach out to those people and ask for support, what do you need from them?

_____

_____

_____

_____

_____

When are you most inspired?

_____

_____

_____

_____

_____

Can you hear your soul's undeniable messages? Why or why not?

_____

_____

_____

_____

_____

In what ways are you dimming your light?

_____

_____

_____

_____

_____

What would your life be like if you said a full-body "yes" to your significance?

_____

_____

_____

_____

_____

In what ways have you been money-focused and money-driven?

_____

_____

_____

_____

_____

_____

What's your big mission in life?

_____

_____

_____

_____

_____

_____

How can you become more mission-driven?

_____

_____

_____

_____

_____

_____

_____

Fear is a liar! How has fear lied to you?

_____

_____

_____

_____

_____

_____

What physical symptoms are you experiencing that are telling you it's time to let something go so you can move on?

_____

_____

_____

_____

_____

_____

How are you owning your life?

_____

_____

_____

_____

_____

_____

In what ways are you NOT owning your life?

_____

_____

_____

_____

_____

_____

How do you know when your soul is speaking?

_____

_____

_____

_____

_____

In what ways do you lead with your ego?

_____

_____

_____

_____

_____

What is your soul's calling?

_____

_____

_____

_____

_____

_____

_____

What do you desire that is outside your comfort zone?

_____

_____

_____

_____

_____

_____

What are you willing to lose to gain everything you desire?

_____

_____

_____

_____

_____

_____

Who are the doubters and naysayers in your life?

_____

_____

_____

_____

_____

_____

Who are the destiny-seekers in your life?

_____

_____

_____

_____

_____

_____

What do you need to believe so you can go out and create magic in your life?

_____

_____

_____

_____

_____

_____

How would you describe what MORE looks like for you?

_____

_____

_____

_____

_____

_____

What special gifts do you have?

_____

_____

_____

_____

_____

_____

What kind of relationship do you have with money?

_____

_____

_____

_____

_____

_____

_____

What lessons have you been taught about money?

_____

_____

_____

_____

_____

_____

How can you use your gifts to make money?

_____

_____

_____

_____

_____

_____

What signs do you see that are telling you it's time to make a move and/
or experience MORE in your life?

_____

_____

_____

_____

_____

_____

What boundaries do you need to put in place so people will respect you and your time?

_____

_____

_____

_____

_____

_____

What do you BELIEVE you deserve?

_____

_____

_____

_____

_____

_____

What is missing from your life?

_____

_____

_____

_____

_____

_____

How do you plan to make a difference in the world?

_____

_____

_____

_____

_____

_____

_____

What have you been chasing in life?

_____

_____

_____

_____

_____

_____

What have you been searching for?

_____

_____

_____

_____

_____

_____

When do you get your best ideas?

_____

_____

_____

_____

_____

_____

_____

What do you do to slow down?

_____

_____

_____

_____

_____

What would inner peace feel like for you?

_____

_____

_____

_____

_____

_____

_____

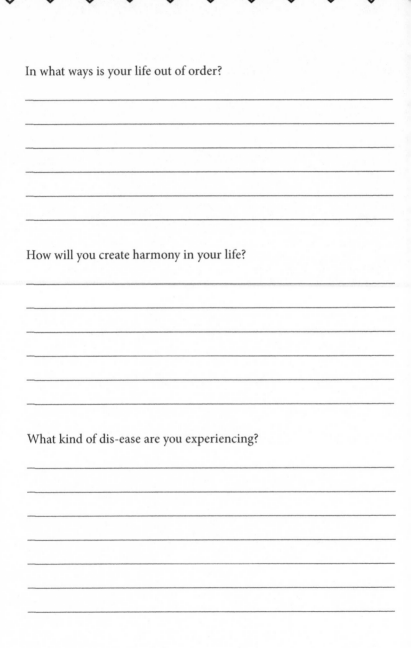

In what ways is your life out of order?

_____

_____

_____

_____

_____

_____

How will you create harmony in your life?

_____

_____

_____

_____

_____

_____

What kind of dis-ease are you experiencing?

_____

_____

_____

_____

_____

_____

_____

How would you describe your current self-love status?

_____

_____

_____

_____

_____

_____

_____

What do you really value?

_____

_____

_____

_____

_____

How would you describe the energy you bring with you?

_____

_____

_____

_____

_____

_____

What kind of energy do you WANT to bring with you?

_____

_____

_____

_____

_____

_____

How will you begin to love yourself better?

_____

_____

_____

_____

_____

_____

What kind of life would you like to wake up to every day?

_____

_____

_____

_____

_____

_____

You have greatness within you; do you know what it is?

_____

_____

_____

_____

_____

_____

What have you overcome that you should celebrate?

_____

_____

_____

_____

_____

_____

What is your big crazy dream?

_____

_____

_____

_____

_____

_____

_____

How can audacity help you live your dream?

_____

_____

_____

_____

_____

Who do you choose to be?

_____

_____

_____

_____

_____

_____

How would you describe what your best version of yourself looks and
feels like?

_____

_____

_____

_____

_____

_____

What about yourself can you honor right now?

_____
_____
_____
_____
_____
_____

What do you love about yourself?

_____
_____
_____
_____
_____
_____

How would you describe your bliss?

_____
_____
_____
_____
_____
_____
_____

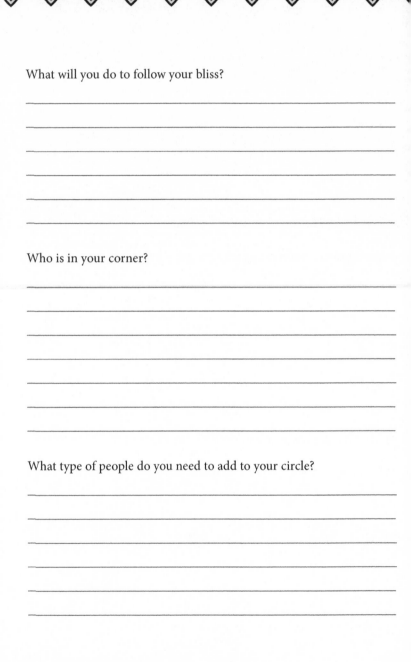

What will you do to follow your bliss?

_____

_____

_____

_____

_____

_____

Who is in your corner?

_____

_____

_____

_____

_____

_____

What type of people do you need to add to your circle?

_____

_____

_____

_____

_____

_____

How has your current level of Emotional Intelligence served you? How has it hindered you?

_____

_____

_____

_____

_____

_____

What makes you feel alive inside?

_____

_____

_____

_____

_____

_____

Who or what is creating misery in your life?

_____

_____

_____

_____

_____

_____

How are YOU creating misery in your life?

_____

_____

_____

_____

_____

_____

What kind of magic do you want to create?

_____

_____

_____

_____

_____

What multidimensional magic lives within you?

_____

_____

_____

_____

_____

_____

_____

In what ways are you speaking DEATH into your life?

_____

_____

_____

_____

_____

_____

In what ways are you speaking LIFE into your life?

_____

_____

_____

_____

_____

_____

What excites your spirit?

_____

_____

_____

_____

_____

_____

_____

What do you seek?

_____

_____

_____

_____

_____

_____

What do you want to do every day for the rest of your life?

_____

_____

_____

_____

_____

What are you here to do?

_____

_____

_____

_____

_____

_____

_____

What is your true calling?

_____

_____

_____

_____

_____

_____

How would you describe what a meaningful life would look like for you?

_____

_____

_____

_____

_____

_____

How do you want to feel for the rest of your life?

_____

_____

_____

_____

_____

_____

How will you use your multidimensional magic to create a meaningful life and to change the world?

_____

_____

_____

_____

_____

_____

In what ways are you playing small?

_____

_____

_____

_____

_____

You have magnificence within you; what does it look like?

_____

_____

_____

_____

_____

What is your destiny?

_____

_____

_____

_____

_____

_____

What kind of legacy will you leave behind?

_____

_____

_____

_____

_____

_____

_____

What are your deepest fears?

_____

_____

_____

_____

_____

_____

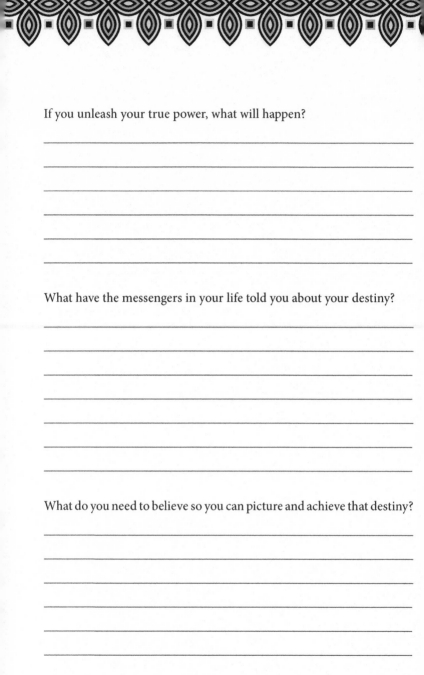

If you unleash your true power, what will happen?

_____

_____

_____

_____

_____

_____

What have the messengers in your life told you about your destiny?

_____

_____

_____

_____

_____

_____

What do you need to believe so you can picture and achieve that destiny?

_____

_____

_____

_____

_____

_____

What will your life be like when you finally unleash your significance?

_____

_____

_____

_____

_____

_____

# Catrice M. Jackson, MS, LMHP, LPC

**INTERNATIONAL ANTI-RACISM EDUCATOR | SPEAKER | AUTHOR | FREEDOM FIGHTER**
America's #1 Expert on White Woman Violence

**CHIEF CONDUCTOR AT HARRIET'S DREAM &
HOST OF BLACK COUCH CONVERSATIONS**

*"Love is rooted in action.
Put your love in motion."*

*Catrice M. Jackson | #Catriceology*

Catrice is a Black woman who loves, centers, and celebrates blackness every day while unapologetically living her best Black life. She is the CEO of Catriceology® Enterprises, LLC; the Chief Conductor at Harriet's Dream®, a racial trauma healing and wellness center for Black women; and the host of Black Couch Conversations, a Black-ass podcast for Black folks with a psychological twist. Catrice is also the creator of SHETalks WETalk Race Talks for Women and the author of more than ten books, including *Antagonists, Advocates and Allies; White Spaces Missing Faces; The Becky Code; Unf\*ckablewith;* and *Weapons of Whiteness™.* As an anti-racism speaker and educator, Catrice serves up strong medicine and hard truths in a straight-up, on-the-rocks, no-chaser style to eliminate the lethal infection of racism. Unbothered by naysayers and unflinching in her approach, Catrice's dedication to Black people is the motivation behind her personal movement, Justice Is Love.

**EDUCATION**

- PhD, Organizational Psychology, Walden University (dissertation in progress).

- MS, Human Services/Counseling, Bellevue University.

- Licensed Mental Health Practitioner (LMHP).

- Licensed Professional Counselor (LPC).

- BS, Criminal Justice Administration, Bellevue University.

- Licensed Practical Nurse, Western Iowa Technical Community College.

- Certified Domestic Abuse and Sexual Assault Advocate, Trainer, and Speaker.

## SOCIAL MEDIA CONTACTS

**FACEBOOK**
@CatriceJacksonSpeaks
www.facebook.com/The-Revolution-Will-Be-Love-105580688176380

| **TWITTER** | **INSTAGRAM** | **YOUTUBE** |
| @Beckyologist | @Catriceology  \|  @thaloverevolution | @Catriceology1 |

## WEBSITES
www.catriceology.com  |  www.catriceologyenterprises.com
www.shetalkswetalk.com  |  www.justicesislovecoalition.com

## RADIO
**SHETALKS WETALK RADIO**
www.blogtalkradio.com/shetalkswetalk

## PODCAST
**BLACK COUCH CONVERSATIONS ON SOUNDCLOUD**
https://soundcloud.com/catriceology

## OTHER CATRICEOLOGY® BOOKS  All Books Sold on Amazon

*Weapons of Whiteness*™
*Unf\*ckablewith*
*The Becky Code*
*White Spaces Missing Faces*
*Antagonists, Advocates and Allies*
*Unleash Your Significance*

*The Billboard Brand*
*Brand Like A BOSSLady*
*The Art of Fear-Free Living*
*Delicious!*
*Soul Eruption!*

## HIRE CATRICE FOR SPEAKING AND EDUCATION

Catrice is available for speaking opportunities, radio and podcast segments, organizational training, anti-racism education, and leadership consulting.